WAR
LOVE YOUR ENEMIES

WAR
LOVE YOUR ENEMIES

RENÉ LAURENTIN

© 1993 Queenship Publishing Company
All rights Reserved

Library of Congress Catalog Card # 94-65099

Published by:
Queenship Publishing Company
P. O. Box 42028
Santa Barbara, Ca. 93140-2028
Phone (800) 647-9882 Fax (805) 569-3274

Printed in the United States of America

ISBN: 1-882972-26-0

TABLE OF CONTENTS

FOREWORD

In Medjugorje, Our Lady came with a message of peace. It is war that came. This was an apparent triumph for opponents and a scandal for superficial believers. Then, faced with the horror that provoked the indignation of the world, the message from Medjugorje, which was said to be commonplace, revealed its originality, depth, and faithfulness to the Gospel - to the point of pardon and love for the enemy.

Medjugorje had irresistibly grown, despite being faced with general repression: repression from Communism and the no less ardent repression from the Bishop himself. This opposition was accepted with patience and respect for the established authorities. This benevolent obedience was rewarded. Dying Marxism was amazed by the deep peace exempt of politicization and by the benefits that the pilgrims brought to the depressed Yugoslavian economy. Shortly before disappearing, from 1987 to 1990, the government finally accepted the visions and assumed them progressively.

As for Mgr. Zanic, Rome rejected his trial of Medjugorje in April 1986 and transferred authority to the Episcopal Conference. But this number one opponent continued to attempt converting his colleagues to his relentless position. Moreover, he went to the parish itself, at the occasion of the 1987 Confirmation, to preach a sermon that did not talk about the Holy Spirit but instead attempted to shoot down in flames this Holy Virgin of Medjugorje, the object of so much love and filial gratitude in the hearts of her listeners. Faced with this inflamed Croatian people which he knows well, the Bishop thought he could give cause to an outcry, a revolt that would allow the condemnation of Medjurgorje as guilty of rebellion. The parishioners felt transfixed but remained heroically calm. They received the cutting words in respectful silence. This was a new and humble victory of faith and obedience to the Church. The Bishop, surprised, concluded that the parishioners had become "indifferent and did not really believe in it any longer." He was mistaken (DN 7, p. 72-76). He received peace and benevolence out of it but still did not cease his opposition up to his retirement in 1993.

After that, many believed a golden age was coming. Croatia was liberated. It had voted for its own independence on the 10th anniversary day of the apparitions. In March 1992, Bosnia-Hercegovina, with Croatians being the majority, also voted, democratically, for its independence. From February 29 through March 29 it became emancipated from the tutelage of the Serbs of Belgrade. This independence was recognized by the United Nation on April 6, 1992.

This feeling of a new age was premature. It did not last long. Serbs defended their hegemony and attacked the state, in which they were a minority, with their powerful armed forces ("the 4th in Europe," it is said). Air raids and tank invasions performed the "ethnic cleansing" of the Croatians and of the Muslims where they were mixed with a Croatian population. The results were murder, concentration camps, expulsions, destruction of churches and houses, and collective rapes orchestrated to "humiliate and debase" the "Croatian race" in its own eyes. Where the Devil can give rise, at the same time, to hate, eroticism, cruelty and injustice, he triumphs. The Holy Virgin had warned that his attacks were severe. The poor emaciated bodies of the prisoners, which were shown on television, are only a small flash of this hell which only the most audacious media would dare show in full.

That which is most important and most impressive was the attitude of the believers. Faced with this horror, a renewal of prayer and fasting asserted itself in Medjugorje and in all of those who live the messages. Vicka and the Franciscans dared preach love for their enemies while asserting that peace came from it. This deep evangelical reaction, which has overcome the impossible, is the best proof given of the authenticity of Medjugorje. Moreover, without fear and without any obstacle stopping them, an immense movement of mutual aid was organized non-stop by the friends of Medjugorje. They brought hundreds of trucks from Italy, France and other countries. These convoys arrived safely thanks to changing, complicated schemes that provided reliable itineraries. These distributions, arranged by private initiative, were more direct (door to door), equitable, efficient and regular than those dropped by the United Nations.

It is time to realize the importance of the event and of the message (of which we only know the visible part). We know that the Medjugorje phenomenon is completed by the secrets, with 7 of them tragic. "Wasn't the civil war one of the secrets?" the visionaries were asked. "No," they answered (separately and unanimously).

Their answer could have been guessed because the 7 secrets mentioned will be preceded, they said, by 3 warnings that appear positive. They specified that the 3rd warning (which is also the 3rd secret) will be a miraculous sign, visible and permanent, that will be given on the hill where the apparitions have occurred.

To want to decipher these secrets is foolish since they must remain hidden for the time being. We only know some major themes about which the visionaries are authorized to talk: our world gives in to sin and disorderly desire polarized by eroticism and drugs, money and power, violence and murder (abortion being the most official and candidly honored one, even though it destroys the heart of the mother along with the child, life and the future).

The world is destroying itself from the inside, and it is from the inside that Our Lady's message wants to restore it. Peace will come only from conversion, prayer and fasting. The message tells us that ecumenism will come only from love, the source of everything. This message is somber. It is serious; however it is not depressing. The visionaries, several of which know the precise date of the catastrophes, are not anxious but instead keep their joy and internal peace because *"All things work for good for those who love God"* (Rm 8, 28). They are above scandal, as if they were being kept from all illusion at the time of triumph.

All of this brings us back to the Church liturgical prayer:

> Come, Holy Ghost, Creator come
> Inspire these souls of thine;
> Till every heart which thou hast made
> Be filled with grace divine.
>
> Thou art the Comforter, the gift
> Of God. and fire of Love
> The everlasting spring of joy,
> And unction from above. [...]

(Hymn 74. C.M.)

1

ON THE WAR BACKGROUND
THE ELEVENTH ANNIVERSARY

The previous volume, published at the time of the eleventh anniversary, was yet able to tell the development of events. This twelfth volume thus starts there.

From glory to war

In contrast to the 10th anniversary, the one with a glorious liberation punctuated by the vote for independence on June 25, 1992, the 11th anniversary occurred against a tragic war background, a double war started by the Serbs who were frustrated in their hegemony:

- Against Croatia, where they not only destroyed the industrial potential but also the church even more, displacing hundreds of thousands of Croatians at the beginning of July 1991.
- Against Bosnia-Hercegovina, which now lives in horror due to non-stop savagery since April 6, 1992.

Under these conditions, the pilgrimages had stopped. Any trip was risky. Medjugorje's sanctuary, which had miraculously escaped destruction, seemed destined to be buried.

Medjugorje protected

The bombs of May 1992, which reached the nearby village of Citluk, were also aimed at Medjugorje. But a bomber pilot who was shot down told the Croatians who retrieved him and his parachute:

-I could not bomb the Church of Medjugorje. If I got close to it, I could not see it anymore: some kind of fog hid it from my eyes.

But, seen from a plane, nothing was easier to spot than its two bell towers.

In short, the first 3 bombs dropped on Medjurgorje fell on muddy ground and did not explode. Then the 6 missiles of May 8 fell on a waste ground 350 meters from the church; these killed only a cow, a dog and a chicken, and damaged an empty house (*Eco* 93 and 95, p. 3b).

This is the story of the bomb that did not explode and that was displayed on the esplanade of the church (an image which is now famous). Apparently at night, a pilgrim took it to the esplanade, but no one knew from where he had gotten this bomb. One day it disappeared in the same anonymous way. I searched for it in vain during my pilgrimage in March 1993. I also inquired at the presbytery and with Sister Emmanuel in order to clarify this curious and deceitful episode.

Father Jozo's appeal

Nevertheless, Father Jozo Zovko, parish priest of Medjugorje when the visions began and founder of the pilgrimage movement, did not just preach in Hercegovania but traveled all over the world to mobilize the authorities. He urged people to renew the pilgrimage, in spite of the storm, in spite of all urgencies and caution. From America, at the Washington National Press Club, he made his appeal for a peace pilgrimage on the date of the eleventh anniversary (June 25, 1992):

ON THE WAR BACKGROUND, THE ELEVENTH ANNIVERSARY

America, I invite you;
Our Lady invites you.
She awaits you:
as pilgrims, as believers,
as those whose only weapon is
the Rosary in their hands.
Let's stop the war.
Let it be the wall against which evil will be brought down.

In order to prepare for the pilgrimage, Father Jozo asked all for nine days of prayer and fasting, from June 16 to June 24, vigil of the official anniversary and beginning of the pilgrimage. The foundation of his appeal rested on Our Lady's message of April 25, 1992:

It is only through prayer and fasting that the war can be stopped.

(Appeal renewed on June 10, 1992, by The Green Ribbon, 193 Twin Drive North East Windsor, NJ 08520. Fax 609443 5354).

That was the first signal for the renewal of the pilgrimage movement, which grew after January 1993.

The peace march (June 24, 1992)

The eleventh anniversary pilgrimage expressed itself through a peace march organized by the Germans for Wednesday, June 24. Two thousand pilgrims took to the road in prayer, from Humac (the Franciscan's novitiate in Hercegovina, near Ljubuski) to Medjugorje: 20 kilometers in a country at war, still under the threat of more bombings. The visionaries, all present for the anniversary, led the march. A radiant Vicka was the figurehead. Archbishop Franic celebrated mass when they arrived...

After the celebration of the anniversary, Father Jozo concluded:

> *Yes, it was a beautiful day, bathed in peace and joy, clothed with prayer. From all parts of Hercegovina, really, as in the past, the pilgrims came here, barefoot, to pay their debt towards their Mother. In our hearts we felt the presence of all of you who decided to remain away; we represented you and prayed for you [...] We have been healed and encouraged. Our prayers were added to yours. Do not be afraid. The table of love and union, prepared by our Mother of Medjugorje, is always ready for you here.*

On the following day, June 25 (the official day of the anniversary according to the vision) at 18:00 hours, Ivanka had her seventh annual vision. She raised her hands. Why? Ivanka explained,

> *The Holy Virgin had lowered hers, and I took them while praying so that the gift of peace would fall upon you. The Holy Virgin was very serious; she advised to intensify prayer to defend ourselves against Satan who wants to destroy us as well as the peace in our heart.*

2

THE NEWS

Now news from Medjugorje comes from a war torn country. Since the Serbs' attempt in May 1992 to destroy this high and symbolic place, Medjugorje has become an oasis of peace again, where "ethnic cleansing" has no meaning since Medjugorje is purely Croatian. The targets are elsewhere.

1. THE VISIONARIES

Ivan

At the beginning of April 1992, when all able bodied men were mobilized, Ivan was drafted to watch out for any aggression and to participate in defensive operations in Mostar and elsewhere. These fighters, who also are faithful, said to Ivan:

- No, your role is to pray, not to use a machine gun.

He took his role seriously. He prays everyday on the Hill of Apparitions.

Appreciated in the USA for his calm, wisdom and humor, he was invited to a long tour, from October 2 to mid-December 1992, and again in 1993.

When he is in Medjugorje, he has, besides his habitual visions, 2 nocturnal visions a week: one, every Monday on the Hill of Apparitions in Podbrdo; the other, on Friday on the Hill of the Cross which dominates Medjugorje 540 meters away in Krizevac.

On the day following the annual pilgrimage, Sunday, September 13, the Holy Virgin warned him that she would not appear to the prayer group for 3 weeks. A similar had happened there during the same time in previous years. (Sister Emmanuel, p. 135).

On January 17, Ivan left with Slavko for a tour of Australia, New Zealand and the Philippines. Crowds of five to seven thousand people (150,000 total) came together to listen to them. Cardinal Edward Clancy presided over these meetings. They came back through Singapore and Vienna on February 23.

I saw Ivan on March 14. Less disturbed by the pilgrims, he works on the family farm. I took notes on the subject of fasting:

I was the first one to receive the message: "Fast on Wednesday and Friday with bread and water." At the beginning, it was very difficult for me. It was a perpetual fight. Now I have adapted. It purifies my soul and strengthens my faith. But fasting is not only about food. You can fast from other things. Fasting is not an end in itself but a means.

To the question: "Vicka said you must love the Serbs. Is it possible for the Croatians?"
He answered:

It is difficult. It is a matter of healing. We must try to heal our wounds. It is not that forgiveness is not possible, but it is difficult to overcome the deepest wounds.

Ivanka

From August 19 to September 29, Ivanka came to the USA for health reasons, along with her husband and their two children. She lives a discreet life in her house, away from the village. She had had to leave her house from April to

June, along with the other mothers and the children, when the worst was feared for Medjugorje.

Jakov

Jakov came to Medjugorje at Christmas time and announced his decision to marry Anna-Lisa Barozzi. The wedding was celebrated by Father Slavko on Easter day (April 11, 1993), in the afternoon. The people were very impressed by the young bride.

To Jakov, whose father died a little before he was ten and whose mother died shortly thereafter, the founding of a family is very important.

Did he experience the apparition on his wedding day? The question was of importance since his Italian hosts had observed that he was not praying at the time the visions would normally have occurred. When asked about it, he answered, "I experience them while I'm praying."

But when? It was not known. Jakov is a very secretive young man. It was said that he had received the 10th secret and that he was no longer receiving visions. On June 23, at the Medjugorje presbyter, I asked him, "It has been said that you do not have visions anymore?"

But I do, of course I do! When I pray, at the times of my choosing.

He had left the Giuliano Pistoni family, with whom he had stayed for a year, in Asola di Mantova. He worked in their sporting goods store. He now lives in Medjugorje where his aunt had a house built for him, right across from Ivan's house.

I had been told that he was thinking about opening a clothing store, probably with help from his Italian host. He told me that he was not. On June 25 he went back to his old job at the parish.

On June 25, I met his young wife Anna-Lisa at her house. She had just returned from a short trip to Italy. She is a very sweet and warm woman. She has made a good impression on everybody. She is a docile spouse, as is expected of a Croatian woman.

Since she met Jakov, she has become more beautiful, Giulano Pistoni told me when I stood next to him during the time of Ivanka's vision.

Marija announces her wedding plans

From May 9 to 22, Marija went on several mission-trips to Italy with Father Orec; from November 12 to 15, she went to Spain and Portugal with Father Slavko.

Between trips, when she was not at home in Medjugorje, she often stayed with her friend Paolo Lunetti in Italy. Since 1988, more and more often, the people of Medjugorje would say, "They will marry." It was also said that her family and the village were against it. Marija was not saying anything about it.

In 1981, she announced that she had chosen a religious vocation. In 1988, with great joy, she left for Parme with Tomislav Vlasic, who was her spiritual guide (DN 8, p. 12; DN 9, p. 20-21). But Paolo, who loved her, was not about to lose her. As often as he could, he would visit her in this religious community theoretically closed to visitors. He also called often. The tension which had erupted between Marija and Tomislav made it easy for him. He finally kidnapped her and made her write a letter in which she expressed her disagreements. Being a wealthy man, in July 1988, he took her on a great trip to Rome, Fatima and Lourdes. Since then, they have rarely been apart and many have wondered why they did not make it official. "Why doesn't she ask the Holy Virgin what she should do: marry or not?" some people said.

But the Holy Virgin does not work like an oracle who dictates the paths of the visionaries. If they consult Her on a specific decision, like a good mother respectful of their freedom, she tells them:

The decision is yours, and it is in prayer that you will see the light.

This explains the long period of incertitude between her earlier years of religious vocation and this persevering protector, a very human man who has revealed to her culture and comfort and who offers to her an easy life and shared love. Marija possesses both strength and fragility and has always needed a strong support in her life.

Finally, Marija (28 years old), accompanied by her future father-in-law Dino Lunetti, announced her decision officially on the Italian station TG4 Buon Pomeriggio (Good afternoon) show. The announcement lasted half an hour and was presented for three days in a row (April 27-29). She repeated what she had often said concerning the message from Medjugorje:

I thought I was made for a religious life. I tried. I failed. So I thought that marriage was my true vocation. The Gospa left me free to make the decision.

As soon as it was announced in Italy, the rumor had it that the wedding would be celebrated privately on May 2, at a convent in Monza. The rumor was wrong. What was true then? Marija has truly decided to marry. She specified on the phone on May 7, 1993:

I became engaged on December 8, the Feast of the Immaculate Conception, But we have not set the wedding date.

In the April 29 issue of *Il Giornale*, Luciano Moia gave an article the title: *The Gospa advised her: "Get married." That was actually saying too much. "What did The Gospa tell you concerning your wedding?"* Marija answered,

> *Nothing. The Gospa lets us be free. She said that we must find answers in prayer. I prayed, and that is how I decided, because being married would allow me more freedom to be a witness. I had wanted to go into a convent but the rules were too strict. I was not able to spend my own time testifying to Mary's messages to the world [...]. You must not forget that Medjugorje represents my whole life.*

Some people also said that her mother was opposed to this wedding. Marija also denied that.

> *My family is more than happy about my decision. My mother had a sister who died young at a convent. To her the monastic life remained tied to her sister's death. She was afraid for me. My father is also very happy.*

A wedding is both good news and the cause for celebration, a time for congratulations to Marija and her fiancee. Then why does this news cause such diverse opinions in Italy as well as in Medjugorje?

The reason is that, from 1981 to 1988, Marija had decided on a religious vocation. For many years, she had been the most ascetic and most heroic of the visionaries. In 1984-1985, before the great celebration of the Holy Virgin, she would fast 3 days a week and sometimes 9 days. These fasts were stopped by doctors because she had been underfed during her childhood, having lived in poverty. Because of this poverty as well as her lucidity, she was compared to Bernadette of Lourdes; Bernadette had been so heroic as to give one kidney to her sick brother at the price of a serious surgery which prevented her from marrying. Marija and Jakov are the first two visionaries who will have married *before the visions were over for them* (as they had been for Ivanka and Mirjana)

Of all the visionaries, she also was the one with the deepest prayer life and a spiritual sixth sense which brought many visitors to see her. She was a symbol up until the day she humbly said, "*Vicka surpassed me.* "It is certainly difficult and constraining for the visionaries to be prisoners of their image, being so often asked to perform the impossible. The disagreements surrounding this wedding were uselessly painful for Marija.

These disagreements are complex. Some think that a visionary should become a nun. But that is not true and is denied by many visionaries. "*I did not believe marriage was a sin,*" said Albert, one of the visionaries from Beauring, to the priests who opposed his engagement, which ended in a happy marriage.

Others are shocked by the fact that Marija, the poorest of the visionaries, should become wealthy. They think of the young rich man in the Gospel who "left sad". But this question of economics is a problem for visionaries whether from Medjugorje or elsewhere. Whether they want it or not, all the people bond together so that they can earn the dividends from their visions. Their fervent admirers offer them sumptuous hospitality and try to materialize their slightest desires: lodging, travel, a pilgrimage to Jerusalem. Each one of them resolves the problem to the best of his ability in a country in distress where everybody survives through aid. If Bernadette declined every gift rigorously, the Bishop of Tarbes provided her father with a decent home and a mill in which he could start his work again. Must we compare this to the hundred fold Jesus promises now in this time to those who have left house or brethren... (Mark 30)?

Some wondered what would happen to Marija's mission if she were going to disappear into this new Italian family protecting her from visitors.

-No, no, that is exactly what I want to avoid. The Holy Virgin chose me to live the message and I am getting married in order to do this. I was not free to do so at the convent. Some people who come here to see may misunderstand.
-But will you live in Italy or in Medjugorje?
-Half and half.
-Paolo agrees?
-Of course.
-And on the 25th, the day of the message, will you rather be in Medjugorje or in Italy?
-I don't know yet. Wait until I am married! (She laughs.)

May the Holy Virgin help her, in her new life, to deepen the quality of her testimony. She and the other visionaries need to pray. Their destiny is not an easy one to follow, especially with so many requests which destabilize their lives. It is almost a miracle that they are able to maintain their stability and this fidelity to their mission.

Mirjana

Mirjana, who had left Medjugorje a year and a half earlier to protect her daughter, came back to Medjugorje in mid-October 1992. On the 2nd day of each month she meets the Holy Virgin, with or without a vision, and prays with her. Mirjana told Sister Emmanuel:

Not only The Gospa prays for the non-believer [which is the constant motivation for their prayers] *but she also suffers much for them. I implore you, pray for them every day, because they do not know what awaits them!*

On her birthday, March 18, Mirjana experienced her 11th annual vision as the Holy Virgin had promised.

For the first time, she said, The Gospa did not mention the secrets' sad perspective. This meeting was pure joy. She was marvelously beautiful. The meeting lasted 7 minutes; and then, I felt like I was in a desert, like one coming back from Heaven (but no one can understand what I am talking about, because they do not know what Heaven's future means). During the vision, she did not forget to pray for the non-believer, those who do not know God's love. The Gospa added another Pater, an Ave and a Gloria for peace in our hearts and the power to convey it to others.

Mirjana received the following message:

My dear children, give me your hand; it is my desire, and like a Mother, I will lead you to the true path and will bring you to the Father. Open your hearts and let me enter. Pray, because in prayer I am with you. Pray, and let me lead you. I am leading you to peace and happiness.

On March 14, 1993, I had asked her:

-In 1984, you had seemed eager to contact Father Petar, the priest chosen to reveal the secrets. Since you already knew it would occur at a later date, why did you contact him so early?
-Father Petar had to prepare himself.

On the same day, one of the pilgrims asked about fasting on Wednesday and Friday:

-Must we eat a little bit of bread or a lot?

-*You must not measure, but you must not take too much.*

To one of the pilgrims who questioned her on a later day:

-On fasting days, can we still drink a cup of coffee with sugar in the morning?

She answered with humor:

-*Yes, but do it quickly before the Gospa wakes up!*

These external casuistries make her smile.

A group of pilgrims who had come with Sabrina Coric questioned her further on her family life:

-*We pray 2 hours a day, me and my husband.*
-How can a husband do so much? One of the pilgrims asked.
-*My husband did not find me in a bag*, she answered literally, according to a popular Croatian saying. (We would say "in a lucky-bag"; in other words he was ready; he knew her religious aspirations very well.)
-*I say the Rosary everyday*, she specified in her home on the morning of June 25, 1993.

Marija, her 2 and a half year old little girl, is very cute and full of life. She was ardently picking flowers before her parents would cut the lawn.

-She prays everyday, Mirjana said. *She lives with the Holy Virgin in her heart and she joins us at the beginning of the prayers: Pater, Ave and Gloria. She already knows how to say them with us.*

Vicka

While all the visionaries are developing into honest people and good Christians, making their own choices in life, albeit at times by trial and error, Vicka, like an arrow thrown straight to the sky, seems ahead of schedule. She gives herself completely to God and humanity: they are the same to her. Since the beginning she is the only one whose vocation has maintained a constant and joyous choice for initiative and the most demanding sacrifice without hesitation or compromise. She is tirelessly available, smiling, glowing with conviction and simplicity. She has entirely devoted herself to being the Gospa's witness. That is why she did not leave Medjugorje at the critical time from April to June, at the time of air-raid warnings and nights spent in a shelter without water or electricity.

In the midst of the storm

During this tragic period, she was tireless in her effort to revive courage and prayer, visiting the ill and distributing aid to the poorest. Every day, she was present during mass celebrated in the basement of the presbyter. She would raise the spirit and faith for all, especially the soldiers whose army uniforms (green and brown) colored the packed crowd.

With her, everything comes from the inside: from the Holy Virgin and the Holy Spirit. Thus she is astonishingly creative and surprising, with the freedom of God's children. During this time, she postponed her appointments with her Swiss doctor and refused or canceled several trips, in particular a tour of Brazil she was supposed to make with Father Orec in

1992... a trip he finally made with Marija in February of 1992.

In June, she noticed how preoccupied the Holy Virgin seemed (*Echo* 93, p. 5). Vicka's cousin asked her:

-Do you remember that you cried when you received the 7th, 8th and 9th secrets, and so did Marija? You say that the secrets do not speak of the war at hand. So what is waiting for us?

You just gave the answer to the question yourself, Vicka answered laconically.

To bear such heavy secrets does not take away her smile or dynamism. She knows that *all things work together for good to them that love God* (Rm 8, 28). It is obvious that it has become second nature to her.

It was recently said that she had cancer (*Informateur*, June 1992). In fact, she only had a benign tumor (removed in the summer of 1991). With her courage and a rare resistance, she seems healthy.

The children's international mobilization

On June 1st, 1992, Vicka started (with her friend's help) a campaign to involve the children of America and the entire world in prayer and sacrifice in order to stop the atrocities committed in this war. She started the campaign with the following letter which was transmitted mostly in the United States and Canada:

Dear children, I have met many of you in Medjugorje, my village, and I love you very much. Now, nobody can come anymore since there is war in my country and everyday, daddies, mommies and children are killed. For-

tunately, the Holy Virgin keeps appearing to us everyday; she has even told us how to stop the war.

Here, in my country, the people say that if the powerful American armed forces came to help us, the war would
be over in one day because our enemies would be very
scared and would go home. But since they are not coming, we have a better idea: you, the small children, will
be this powerful army that will come to stop the war in
our homeland. OK?

Above all do not be afraid, because you will have the
kindest and most powerful Queen in the world to lead
you: the Holy Virgin. But of course you will need good
quality weapons that do not miss. There is no need to
buy them, because in our visions, the Holy Virgin told us
that the best weapons are hidden in each one's heart. And
do you know what these weapons are? They are prayer
and sacrifice: sacrifice from the heart. Those are the most
powerful weapons in the world against war and evil. The
Holy Virgin is saddened by this war. Especially in this
country in which She has chosen to appear. I see it on
Her face. She loves us so much! She told me she was
looking for her children to help her with these two weapons, and that if they truly accepted to help her, then she
could stop the war. She needs you; do you want to help
her?

Write your answer: yes or no. If you write yes, then
here is how to show the Holy Virgin that you belong to
her army. Everyday, you will use these two weapons by
saying a prayer with all your heart and also by making
a small sacrifice that will cost you. With each prayer
and sacrifice, you will color a drawing, and when you
will have finished your drawings you will send them to
me. I will give them to the Holy Virgin. To Her it will be
the sign that you have worked very hard with Her towards victory.

Here are the drawings. In each drawing (there were 8 of them), *there are eight parts you can fill each time you have prayed or made a sacrifice. Of course you may pray several times a day, or make several sacrifices; this way your drawing will be sent to the Holy Virgin sooner.*

Then Vicka explained each image:

The first drawing is a MIG bombing our country. There are 7 bombs. Each time you can color a bomb you help the Gospa, and she stops the bomb from falling on us [...].

The eighth drawing is our beautiful church in Medjugorje, where the Gospa has often come to pray with us and where so many pilgrims have received gifts from her. Each time you fill one part you help the Gospa in protecting Her church against bombardments, and also the other churches in our country.

Of course, you can suggest to your big brothers and sisters to join the Gospa's army. And all your friends everywhere.

I thank you from the bottom of my heart for your help, and I hope that after the war, you will be able to come with your parents to Medjugorje, because the Holy Virgin invites us all.

In Rome

On September 20, 1992, during a brief visit to Rome, she addressed this exhortation to the group Queen of Peace:

Mary's messages apply to the whole humanity. They are concerned with prayer, conversion, fasting, penitence and peace. The Gospa asks us to say the rosary's joyous, sorrowful and glorious mysteries everyday. She asks us to fast with bread and water every Wednesday and Friday, but she mostly ask us to have a strong faith. To those who are ill, the Holy Virgin asks to give up something precious for her; but to us who are healthy, she asks for fasting with bread and water. Finding excuses such as "My head hurts or my stomach hurts" is only the weakness of our will. If we accept fasting with love we will also have the strength of living it. On the subject of conversion, the Gospa said:

-When you are in trouble, disagreement and pain, you think Jesus and I are far away from you. On the contrary,

Mary assures us that Jesus and she are always with us. She asks us to open our heart and life to better know how much they love us. She asks us to give up something dear to us, but Mary's greatest joy is when we renounce sin. She gives her love and peace to each one so that we become the bearers and the givers in the places we live.

On the subject of family life, she has asked that we begin by saying the rosary within one's family and in communities. [...]

She also tells us how strong Satan is and that his aim is to confuse us. Thus she asks us to intensify our prayers [...] Mass must be in first place because it is the most sacred and most important moment in our life. Mass is when Jesus comes among us to live in our heart [...] She also asks us to confess at least once a month and to fast every week. (Echo 97, p. 4b.)

At the center of Sister Elvira's recovering addicts

Sister Elvira, who has founded a number of centers for recovering addicts, invited Vicka to visit Lourdes with her where she wants to establish a new house, her 18th under the Holy Virgin's aegis. The houses are managed by the recovering addicts themselves. They pray three hours a day and do not watch television. Mother Theresa asked that other foundations be started in Florida and Calcutta.

Sunday morning, November 29, Vicka was present for the mass in the "Grotto". She experienced her visions secretly after Communion because ecstasy is not to draw attention to oneself; no one seeing her face turned towards the altar would have made her a prioress among others.

During the day, she visited several convents that wanted to know her (Dominicans, Clarisses, Visitandines). In one of them where there were some reservations about Medjugorje, their judgment became positive. From 3 to 5 o'clock in the afternoon, Vicka met with a prayer group in one of the houses and said the rosary; she then prayed for those who wished her to do so.

On Monday, November 30, Sister Elvira had already found a space and was preparing for a trip at the end of February to close the deal. Vicka left from the Ossun airport on Monday at 1 o'clock in the afternoon after praying for a handicapped child who had been brought to her from Tarbes.

Love for the enemies

Vicka's most remarkable virtue is her forgiveness for the enemy. From the beginning of the war, at the time which was most threatening, she said,

> *In these tragic times, we must feel compassion for the Serbs. What can a people do when it is deprived of God, love and values, and has an ideal inculcated forcefully by hate propaganda? The ferocity of the aggression [...] shows that it is the instrument of a superior homicidal power [...].*
> *Yes, we must show compassion for all and pray so that peaceful thoughts find a way into their hearts [...]. The*

*persecutors are more unfortunate than the ones perse-
cuted and attacked.*

And she concludes by citing the Gospel: *"Father forgive
them [...] Love thy enemies [...] If thy enemy is hungry, give him
food"* (Eco, June 1992, NO. 93, p.5).

In September she confirmed,

*When the Gospa asks us to pray, it is meant for any
man, whoever he might be: Serb or Muslin, friend or
enemy. If we do not show him that we love him and pray
for him, if we do not give the example of loving and for-
giving, this war will not end.*

*It is important for us not to think about revenge. If
we said, "one did wrong, he must pay", we would be doing the same thing he does and the war will never end.*

*We must forgive and say, "We pray for the Serbs be-
cause they do not truly know what they do." May our
prayers reach their hearts, and may they understand that
this war does lead anywhere* (Echo. NO. 93, p. 3b).

On November 23, Vicka told Alberto Bonifacio:

*The major problem is not fear of war; it is inside us,
because there is so much hate in our hearts. Today this
hate between the Croatian people and the Serbian people
is openly expressed. Thus we must clear our hearts and
our souls. Only then peace will come. Until our hearts
are purified, peace will certainly not come. And this true
is for all, not only for our people.*

*We cannot say that the Serbs sin and that we do not.
No! We are all the same.*

On top of this a politician comes. He starts to talk and then what happens? Always war against one another. It is not God's fault. We all are His children. So the Gospa says that we all are brothers and sisters to God. There are no Serbs or Croatians or Italian. There are only His children. I want good things for all. The Gospa says that our words are useless. Only our prayer and our example can move our hearts.

Jelena

Jelena, invited by the extremely fervent University at Steubenville to pursue her studies, has returned to Medjugorje for the Christmas holidays. This 20 years old student, now fluently trilingual, surprised her friends by sharing her last discovery:

-*During her terrestrial life, the Holy Virgin never stopped saying the Rosary.*

-How! She would have said the Ave Maria to herself each day?

-*Of course not! But she always meditated on Jesus' life, and her internal gaze never abandoned her. Don't the Rosary's 15 mysteries make us relive in our heart Jesus' entire life...and also Mary's? Such is the Rosary's true spirit. It is not only a matter of reciting the Ave.*

Everyday Jelena receives inner locutions accompanied by images or intimate visions. She appears to get deeper and deeper into a profound contemplation... in spite of her studies. But Steubenville is not a university like the others. It is a praying university. Two thirds of the students spontaneously go to mass everyday.

The visionaries, pulled apart at the beginning of the war, gather more and more often in Medjugorje. They were all there at Christmas and then around the end of February. Jakov moved there after his wedding. They all have their home at Medjugorje.

2. THE FRANCISCANS

The Franciscans uphold the message like a torch while committing themselves to welcoming refugees and distributing relief supplies to the parishioners.

At a time when the war was raging, Jozo Zovko left for a great international 43 day tour, beginning in May until June 22 1992, the date of his return to Zagreb. He received an unequaled and eager welcome from divers governments. He tells us a little about the beginning of his trip:

I talked to Lord Carrington about the sin of omission, the cross we have to bear, the design for the great Serbia that pushes its leaders to aggression.

"I am not God, I cannot stop the war. Europe cannot either," he answered me.

Every night in London, I met many pilgrims and some Anglicans too, and we prayed together. The Anglican Bishop had been to Medjugorje. He told me: *"I believe it."* He helped me a lot with the organization of my meetings.

It is Lord Carrington who sent me to New York and to the United Nations, being the only place from which an efficient decision could come. Catholics and Protestants both helped me. They organized many meetings, including with the Security Council. I asked them for an examination of conscience: *"It is not one million but 2,200,000 people who have no roof over their heads."* I told them about the invader's barbarity leaving the land destroyed, devastated: 700 churches, monasteries and cemeteries - reduced to ruins by bombs.

Well! That did not shake them up. But the Holy Virgin remained my consolation.

At the United Nations, Moslems applauded when I said, *"Here the Holy Virgin appeared."* They, in Bosnia, have the greatest tolerance for our religion; whereas Serbs destroy the mosques as well as the churches.

At the Security Council, I said, *"It is possible to stop the war."*

"We do not know how," they answered.

"We must pray and fast. Don't you see that Europe is already at war?" (Echo no. 94, p. 5).

On June 10, in Notre Dame de Paris, France, Father Slavko said:

Your reaction when confronted with world events shows a sign of dechristianization. A good Samaritan's reaction would be different [...]. The war started in man's heart; that France, Belgium, and Germany are asked for an examination of conscience is not surprising. Like the Priest and the Levite who went from Jerusalem to Jericho, these nations met a man who was hurt but not dead, but who was most likely to die. He asked for help, but they kept going their way. They were going up to the Temple. Now, the Gospa asks us to examine our conscience to see if we know how to love and bear our neighbor's cross. But do we know ourselves how to bear our cross? It is not simply Bosnia-Hercegovina that is at war but the whole of Europe, at war with itself, because it does not know how to love.

Father Jozo came to Rome on June 17, 1992. He met John-Paul II during a general audience:

"Take care of Medjugorje, do not renounce, but persevere. Be brave, I am with you," the Pope told him (Echo no. 95, p. 3a).

He told the Romans:

I came here to ask you to pray. If we, the Church, have lost God, we must make Him our priority again. If Rome, the center of Faith, abandons prayer, who can become the faithful? Mary cries when she speaks of us priests; we are hard. It is easier to sit in front of the television that in front of the tabernacle. Pray for the priests; pray for us so that we can remain faithful and announce the only way Christ is. Christ awaits us. Devote yourself and your family to His Heart. I thank you all because you want peace. To get it, put in practice Mary's message.

WAR: LOVE YOUR ENEMIES

3

INVESTIGATIONS AND POSITIONS IN THE CHURCH

This year, my annual chapter on the Medjugorje investigations has been reduced to its simplest expression. The urgencies of the war have interfered with my work and that of any private or official investigation. Monsignor Komarica, President of the Investigation Commission, is not free in his movements and could not go to the colloquium of the Journal La Croix to which he was invited in April. He has been practically placed under house arrest in his Diocese, in Banja Luka, where ethnic purification by the Serbs is raging. Although his life is threatened, he nevertheless preaches peace to his people, while standing up to the inflexible adversary who cuts down so many lives.

Destroyed Archives

The town of Mostar was destroyed: bridges, destroyed or damaged; the Bishop's residence, set on fire with no water to fight the flames.

Faced with these devouring flames, I could see Satan at work, said Monsignor Zanic. *I took refuge in the Cathedral. Only God can save us.*

A 30,000 book library and the archives, including those of the Medjugorje investigations, were destroyed. After the confiscation of the presbytery's archives by the police on August 15, 1981, this represents another loss in the history of the apparitions. More and more human and material destruction makes Mostar a martyr town no less than Sarajevo.

The attitudes toward Medjugorje remain the same. The pilgrimages have been accepted (DN 10, p. 19-30; DN 11, p. 41-49), but the bishops did not take charge of them as it was planned because there have been so few pilgrims. This transition is providential. Monsignor Zanic, a member of the Episcopal Commission created to investigate Medjugorje's grace, so fertile in conversions, was himself preparing to multiply restrictions in order to stifle these pilgrimages. A draft had already been written for that purpose but was not published. The war took care of these restrictions beyond anything expected. The crowd fell from more than a million pilgrims each year to less than 100,000 in 1992, with a time in the Spring of 1992 when there were none.

A new bishop in Mostar

Monsignor Zanic, Bishop of Mostar, reached the age limit of 75 years old on May 20, 1993, but was able to prepare for his succession during his longs trips to Rome in the Spring of 1992. For a long time he has had a network of friends in high places who allowed him to choose his coadjutor and successor, the Director of the Croatian College Saint-Jerome in Rome, Monsignor Ratko Peric.

The new bishop is a man of value, a theologian born in Rovisce on February 2, 1944. He studied philosophy in Zagreb then theology in Rome. Ordained as a priest on June 29, 1969, he received his doctorate in dogmatic theology in Rome, was named parish priest, then professor at the Seminary of Dubrovnik and at the Faculty of Theology of Sarajevo. In 1979, he became Rector of the Croatian College in Rome. He was chosen by the Pope to become Bishop of Mostar on June 11, 1992 while he was not yet 50.

Mostar's Cathedral, being reduced to walls with no roof, could not receive the Episcopal Ordination. Thus the new bishop was ordained in Neum, near the Adriatic, on September 12, 1992.

Monsignor Peric shares Monsignor Zanic's opposition to the apparitions (a fact that Bishop Zanic kept in mind in his support of this successor). Rumor suggested that he was "even more opposed", but that seems to be an exaggeration of the facts. (Rumors travel fast among Medjugorje's network of friends.)

Nevertheless, the diocese and pilgrims responded to his selection with dispositions of total obedience, trust and respect, the same response they awarded to Monsignor Zanic, their former Bishop, successor of the Apostles. They trust the Virgin Mary in giving him the light that has converted so many pilgrims in Medjugorje and that is shared by John Paul II himself.

We welcome the new pastor with love and support him with prayer, Sister

Emmanuel wrote at the time of the consecration in Neum.

The new bishop is a man who is calmer, less impulsive, and more moderate than Monsignor Zanic. He avoided all negative declaration. Asked by *Mondadori Video News* for the audio-cassette *Medjugorje oggi: la voce della speranza* (Medjugorje today: the voice of hope):

-Do you believe in the Madonna's apparitions in Medjugorje?

He answered:

-I feel great gratefulness towards Our Lord for his ability to communicate to men through His messages, especially through His Mother. And I would like to thank the Italian public opinion for its humanitarian and concrete aid

given to our people: to the millions of refugees, victims of total destruction [...]

-Which miracle should be asked of the Madonna?

-Certainly, like them, I would asked for peace, because it is the greatest gift Our Lord can give us.. And thus, He did not only leave Himself in the Eucharist, but He also left us peace: "I leave you peace, I give you peace." Assuredly, we compromise this peace by our behavior, but we would like to have it. We would like to experience and live it, especially in our present days. We have so much need for it. (Echo no. 100, p. 8).

In all of this, Monsignor Peric has carefully avoided taking a position for or against Medjugorje. Clearly he approaches Medjugorje with a predominant concern for peace.

After his ordination in Neum, a journalist interviewed him and published his answers in *Slobodna Dalmacija* (Split), on October 6, 1992.

-Question.- At the end of the ordination ceremony, Bishop Zanic especially recommended unity and good feelings within the clergy. Would this not be because of the Hercegovina problem [the dissension between the Franciscans, 80% of the clergy, and the secular, 20%], and the misunderstandings tied to the Holy Virgin's apparitions in Medjugorje? Today, how do you see the solutions?

-Mgr. Peric.- In principle, both questions are settled. Now we must put them in practice reasonably and with love.

-The first case was settled in 1975 by the Holy See's decision, or, more precisely, by the Holy Father: the repartition of the parishes in Mostar's bishopric.

-The second case, Medjugorje, was settled with the shared declaration by the Croatian bishops in Zadar on April 10, 1991, that was not contested by the Holy See.

-Medjugorje's supernatural characteristics could not be proved, and no one is called or able to cut off even one letter from these decisions. I would not want this to be interpreted as rigidity, but as the Church's decision which must be respected. The Church is based on obedience to the hierarchy and on faith. Nothing can put her in difficulty as much as disobedience, discord or her rebellious children. And nothing gives her a proof of love and an aureole of light better than obedience. I know that obedience is not a modern notion; but if I were encouraging something else, I would move away from obedience to Christ and the Holy Spirit.

"The Bishop urges obedience to the bishops' negative decision," some interpreters told me. "This presages an action opposed to Medjugorje." "No," I answered, "because the bishops' decision is not negative." It is positive; they have officially recognized the pilgrimage. The Bishop, President of the Episcopal Commission, Monsignor Komarica, came to celebrate the pilgrimage mass in the name of all the bishops "including Monsignor Zanic" (which he specified). Being the bishop of the area, Monsignor Zanic took his turn in celebrating with The Archbishop of Sarajevo. This finished the consecration of the pilgrimage establishing its legitimacy and the responsibility of the Episcopal Conference as mandated by Rome. Thus the pilgrimage cannot anymore, in any way, be considered an act of deviance or disobedience, according to the thesis Monsignor Zanic could never accredit. The Bishop still lives in hope that his opinions will prevail, but this does not presage any open opposition.

The document dated April 10, 1991, evoked by Monsignor Peric, has clarified the ambiguous text of the first draft that was published tendentiously by the adversaries on January 3, 1991. This text states a double declaration:

> *-The supernatural characteristic (in the miraculous sense) is not established, but is not excluded either; the Episcopal Commission continues its work to get to a decision, a decision the bishops do not want judged prematurely.*
> *-The pilgrimage, of national and international dimension, is the bishops' responsibility.*

This interpretation of Monsignor Peric's decision was recently confirmed. In March, Father Ivan Landeka, parish priest of Medjugorje, met the Bishop who listened for a long time and without criticism to his point of view. He announced his coming to the Confirmation on June 6, 1993, and asked Father Ivan:

> - What do you want from me?
> - *Be yourself,* he answered.

He sent his report and on that base the Bishop will necessarily send him his orders.

His feeling is that the new Bishop is a man of peace and stability who wishes to channel fruitful pilgrimages with discernment, in dialogue with the Franciscans. The outcome of this would most likely be the end of the insidious war in Medjugorje.

There is no more war with the Communists who are gone; there is no more tension with Monsignor Zanic who has prematurely retired. At the beginning of Spring 1993, a few months before the official age limit of retirement (which for him was May 20), Monsignor Zanic was hospitalized for heart problems in Split, his original diocese. His operation was successful. He will remain in Split. We wish him a good convalescence and good rest after such hard work and su~ ships.

On Sunday, May 12, in the Cathedral (with breaches from the bombings), Monsignor Peric sealed the reconciliation with the Provincial Franciscan Fra Drago Tolj who celebrated it with him. Together, they signed a letter that hopes to end "a long murderous war" and to establish a full pastoral collaboration. The Franciscans acknowledge the recent decision that established 4 parishes in Mostar and that had once been viewed like another act of war. The new Bishop is engaged in ecumenism and has published on this subject. Open to dialogue, he right away contacted the Orthodox and Muslims in his diocese:

-*We ask that the Catholics not to destroy our mosques,* the Muslim chief told him.

-*Certainly, but the Muslims must no longer adhere to the maxim: 'War on Christ,'* the bishop answered.

The dialogue is not easy since the offensive against the Croatians of Mostar. The Bishop's work is particularly delicate since, in each community, the religious chiefs have little influence on the military chiefs.

Healing

With regards to a chapter on miracles, no *work* can be mentioned at this point. Doctor Korljan's death, in Split on May 19, 1992, was a loss for Medjugorje. This psychiatrist was a valuable man in all scientific, political and familial fields. He was the founder of *The Croatian Party* which played a role in the liberation and the first steps of an independent Croatia. Feeling his health declining, he chose not to be a candidate for the elections; he was only the president of this democratic party.

He perfectly directed the scientific work on Medjugorje with which the Episcopal Commission had entrusted him, and the conclusions he soundly established were completely positive:

> - the visionaries' perfect psychic health, including Vicka, whom a few doctors had mistakenly contested.
> - the extraordinary value of Damir Coric's recovery, who had been selected among many for a thorough checkup (DN 10, P. 36-37).

Although they were never published, I was aware from him of the quality of his work and the clarity of his conclusions. Why the bishops' declaration never mentioned these is difficult to understand. Doctor Kroljan's work could have guided the doubtful conclusions of the Commission into a more positive direction.

Why this silence? On one hand, the scientific commission has always been treated like a poor relation. It was a marginal group, kind of a lesser commission; and its president, although an officially appointed, well-known man of science, never sat with the group that was essentially theological. The president does not seem to have been replaced after his death (May 19, 1992) which had been preceded by months of decline and illness.

But the principal cause for this obscurity was the episcopal solidarity behind Monsignor Zanic whose powerful opposition prevented any even slightly positive declaration.

The private commission of Italian doctors, founded by Luigi Farina, did not communicate new conclusions since the ones I had obtained unofficially and published in DN 10, p. 36-40.

But healing still happens. I will talk about this in the chapter on testimonies.

From the bishops

The bishops' pilgrimages, more than a hundred in 1991, stopped when the war started. But the fruits of Medjugorje continue to impress many of them. Many welcome the visionaries, including Cardinal Clancy in Sydney, Australia.

Cardinal Kuharic himself, Primate of the Croatian Church, when questioned by the Medjugorje prayer group from Vienna, answered:

> *Those who believe, in good faith, are convinced that through the diffusion of the messages they can stimulate others to good, conversion and peace. In fact it is a question of conscience.*

In September of 1992, the Bishop of Strasbourg gave permission to Monsignor Paul Hnilica to speak on Medjugorje in one of the largest churches in town. Monsignor Hnilca reported:

> The church was full; prayer, fervent. Some stayed from 1500 [3:00 p.m.] to 2300 [11:00 p.m.]. From the people's testimonies who were present, the fruits of this prayer were intense. The vocations that are notably its result seem to have convinced the town bishop more than any speech would have.

The bishop asked him about "the greatest spiritual movement existing today".

As for the Pope, we have cited the numerous bishops he encouraged to make the pilgrimage to Medjugorje (DN 10, p.95-96). The Polish Sister who takes care of his apartments said to Father Jozo Zovko:

-The Pope reads l'*Echo de Medjugorje*. We give him the one we receive in Polish.
-On March 14, in the *Angelus*, he spoke of the fasting and prayer the Holy Virgin asks of Medjugorje. He emphasized these, as well as Father Orec.

John-Paul II continues to manifest his discreet sympathy; he remains (according to government principles) totally respectful of the feelings and responsibilities of each position within the Church. To an Italian who begged him to put an end to Monsignor Zanic's opposition, he answered in the following way:

-*He is the judge of his actions.*
-But you are his judge?
-*No, his judge is God.*

SUPPLEMENT

JOHN PAUL II ON THE WAR
A TEXT DISTORTED AND
VILIFIED BY THE PRESS

The press had done very little about the Pope's previous appeals. But when it found John Paul II's letter to the Bishop of Sarajevo dated February 2, 1993, the press pounced upon it. In the letter the Pope talked, among other things, about the collective rapes perpetrated by the army and the Serbian militia, without mentioning the country so as to not add fuel to the fire.

For example, here is how *La Republica,* dated February 7,1993, titled its first page:

Wojtyla without pity
"Women raped in Bosnia, do not have an abortion."
An act of war against women.

Despite the quotation marks, the Pope's quotation is by no means literal. It is not meant for these women. He does not order them. He places this problem in a drama that he would like to see peacefully resolved. Many have asked me to publish this "unobtainable" text mostly known by summaries grossly distorted. Here it is.

The Pope starts by testifying to his compassion for the "sufferings of the pastors and the populations of Bosnia-Hercegovina" subjected to this "material and spiritual devastation that goes on and on". He emphasizes the "privations" that especially affect "the children".

He wants to mobilize the families, "sanctuaries of life and love", into an "effort towards peace by creating opportunistic initiatives" about which he is not precise since they can only be invented within the situation. That is when he invites the pastors and the faithful, with familial and pastoral responsibility, to take charge of the situations in which the mothers, spouses and young women who have been subjected to violence stemming from racial hatred and brutal lust find themselves.

> *These people who have been the object of such grave violence must find support, understanding and solidarity in the community.*

After this he comments, without using the imperative and forbidden style that the press indicates, on his profound recommendation concerning this deplorable and inextricable drama. He emphasizes:

> *Even in such a painful situation, we must help them to distinguish between the blameworthy act of violence done by men without reason and conscience, and the reality of the new human beings who have come to life anyway. These new creatures, images of God, must be respected and loved in the same way as all other members of the family. It must be reaffirmed in every case, with the most clarity, that the newborn, not bearing any responsibility for what happened, is innocent and thus cannot be, in any way, considered an aggressor. Consequently, the whole community will have to support these women, so painfully hurt, as well as their family, in order to help them in transforming an act of violence into an act of love and welcoming.*

Beyond these particularly atrocious and revolting cases, the Pope emphasizes to the whole world a duty for reconciliation beyond racism and a duty to help those who have been materially and morally hurt by violence and hatred.

The Gospel reminds us that we must not follow an act of violence by an act of violence (Mt 5, 38-41). To the barbarity of hatred and racism, we must answer with the power of love and solidarity. Did not the Apostle Paul recommend to the early Christians who were persecuted by a hostile power: "Do not repay anyone evil for evil; be concerned for what is noble in the sight of all. ... Do not be conquered by evil but conquer evil with good"? (Rm. 12, 17 & 21) I am certain that other Churches, not only in Europe but also in all parts of the world, will know how to find ways to help the people and the families in these situations which carry such grave material, psychological and spiritual difficulties. I encourage with all my heart these goodwill initiatives while keeping in mind Christ's word: "Whosoever receives one child such as this in my name, receives me" (Mark 9, 37).

John Paul II then invites us to promote the adoption of these children who would be abandoned, because the Pope knows very well that in such conditions, the psychological acceptance of the child is often insurmountable. Thus the Pope concludes:

> *Finally, in the case of orphans or abandoned children, I want to address a word of assurance to all who try hard to encourage adoption procedures: when these little ones lose the support of those who gave them birth, to offer them the warmth of a new home is a gesture of great human and Christian value.*

The Pope's appeal stimulated the already established Association *Pour l'adoption des orphelins de Croatie* which has extended itself to these unwanted children, born as the result of the horrible and sacrilegious wound of a rape. At the beginning of 1993, Father Jozo thanked people for the 2,000 adoptions already made (Eco 102, p. 6c). This organization does the impossible in answering the unstoppable growing demands.

39

The Pope finishes by reassuring this Church and these stricken people of the solicitude and the solidarity of the Roman Church which "presides in charity".

This text shocks modern sensibility. But the Pope considers it his duty to defend *Human Rights* according to God's law. Our civilization defends them, in theory, with passion on lesser points, but cheerfully violates them in many ways as soon as these rights become a bother.

The *Comite ethique francais* has acknowledged that Human Rights start at the origin: at the beginning of human life with its formidable and irresistible dynamism. But in our country where abortions are a banality, justified and subsidized, where the public of one of our good French towns gave an ovation to a father who had killed his little daughter with scissors and who was triumphantly acquitted, the *Comite ethique* is challenged by the Parliaments that send its texts to the garbage cans. We have remained savages, more savage than the savages on certain points. The Pope is ahead on the absolute rights of man made in God's image whatever the cost. He does not condemn those who violate these rights, but invites every individual to respect them.

- *Woe betide the Pope if he remains silent for fear of the media*, John Paul II recently said.

4

RECESSION OF POLEMICS

The war has also calmed the polemics. It seemed to curtail pilgrimages so well that the polemicists lost interest in the overturn of these adversaries. Some instead began aiming their weapons at Vassula Ryden, the visionary residing in Switzerland, whose world apostolate has caused such a large prayer and conversion movement. The inquisitors' virus is not dead; the tempter still awakens it within good Christians in surprising but very explainable ways. The prince of darkness is agile at capturing fervent Christians with their good values. Some deviate towards secular ideologies. For others, the ecumenical concern turns to indifference; others pervert the legitimate critical concern for discernment into ruinous demystification. Just recently, a Medjugorje convert, a young gifted child with several diplomas, applied to a high place of theological teaching in order to deepen his faith. No luck! In the first class on exegesis the professor started by saying:

-*Today we are going to study the Marriage in Cana. We must say right away that it is a legend.*

At that point, a student monk intervened with poise:

-And what about the Resurrection?
-*On that issue, we must be very careful,* the professor answered. *We will talk about it again.*

The young ex-graduate of the Ecole Polytechnique, who went there to deepen his faith, withdrew his candidature and went to find the light somewhere else.

Others, on the contrary, with a laudable desire to defend the Faith and the Dogma against so many regrettable losses, become narrow-minded inquisitors concerned with slashing the errors that, in fact, are legion. Curiously, their ardor for the purity of faith does not fight against errors of deviant theologians but against fervent people, especially against the visionaries whose prophetic, non-conventional language is sometimes vulnerable. Medjugorje and Vassula were the principal targets of these new inquisitors.

A few polemicists remain faithful to their convictions, and some speak up once in a while. Abbot Grumel, "priest according to the Order of Melchisedech", often writes to me with courtesy but without concession. His position has been firm since 1984 without needing to go to Medjugorje or knowing any of the visionaries. I cannot but admire his perseverance.

Belanger (who no longer teaches at the University of Montreal) remains silent. We do not know why he did not publish the second volume which he had announced was imminent in the mid-eighties.

Michel de la Trinite, from the *Contre Reforme,* has made a fresh start. He joined the Chartreux to lead a contemplative life united with God beyond any polemic. But he left his papers and notes with his previous community that consciously exploited this gold mine, as we had already mentioned in DN 10, p. 42, 62 and 11, p. 57-59.

Inquisition always pursues its prey. In February 1992, no 280, p. 27, it published a perfectly tendentious report of an opposing pilgrim's non-pretentious "testimony" that the apparitions had remained impassive.

The latest News 11, in which I spoke very objectively about the peaceful meetings between Monsignor Zanic and his adversaries as well as the visionaries, irritated the polemicists who had no words severe enough to depreciate this " charming operation ", this "door-to-door selling" (because the meeting occurred in the Bishop's Palace in Mostar). The meetings did not mean anything in that "the bishop has not changed his mind and that he is courteous". That's what I was telling myself, without feeling any rage. They say it again, seasoned with their homemade vitriol. In his efforts for Christian peace, all would be vacuous, a "total void", the polemicists conclude.

According to them, I should have been dismayed by the fact that Monsignor Zanic had been warmly embraced by Sister Lucie. This fact would be "highly significant" because it would manifest that "the visionary of Fatima encourages the Bishop to maintain his negative position". In fact, this warm embrace, as Brother Augustin says, without concern for morality, is pure invention. So why would I be embarrassed by this formidable objection that is false and that simply lacks any established foundation in reality?

According to the polemicist the apparitions in Medjugorje would be grotesque, with "crazy laughs", grimaces, etc. - an opinion that thousands of witnesses and hundreds of videos refute. In fact, the polemic remains stranger to the facts and to discernment as well as to the fruits and to the work of God.

La Contre Reforme inspired Michele Reboulk (usually inclined to better inspirations) to write an article published in *Monde et Vie* (July 1992, No.. 133, p. 11) that swims in the same waters. She artistically covers the anti-Medjugorje book, which criticism will be found in DN 10, p. 42-62. There is nothing new here besides the style. There really are some "conversions" in Medjugorje, the article concludes. Quite simply the devil, a great tactician, "prefers to lose a little in order to gain a lot". He has encouraged prayer, conversions and the many vocations issued from Medjugorje to devaluate the Virgin of Fatima.

The article is filled with falsehoods more or less defamatory and futile, as previous volumes have already shown. The *Renouveau charismatic* and "complete" takeover by hotheads from this movement are respectable and respected, but are the black sheep of *La Contre Reforme,* because their fervor drives away potential recruits:

> *Medjugorje's Franciscans are violently opposed to their Provincial and Bishop, and have been for quite a long time,* it is still said.

However, the contrary is true. Obedience and respect have remained constant in very difficult conditions. The Bishop and the Provincial have always been received honorably and amiably to the presbyter table. Some have to continue to repeat those calumnies if they want to prove that the work of God comes from the devil. These sincere, thus respectable, polemicists' point in common is that they never went to see what they talk about. They work from a jumble of distorted texts which they take after again and again while distorting them a little bit more each time, like these kids who play at stealing chewing gum full of each one's saliva.

It is useless to insist on these points anymore. Many readers of *Dernieres nouvelles 10 et 11* reproached me for this chapter on the polemic: "Do not bring yourself down to this level of trash", they wrote me. But other Medjugorje pilgrims, impressed by those seemingly pious and scientific criticisms, ask for these to be settled. Like *Le meunier, son fils et l'ane,* I look for a conciliatory solution: to point out the errors without losing myself in the polemic. But let's not stay anymore on this painful chapter.

At a time when the inquisitors are getting tired, we are surprised to find flourishing extremely favorable articles where we least expected. Robert Serrou has published in Paris Match of December 31 a courageous article that casts no shadows. *La France Catholique,* that rejected any information coming from me because of grave and mysterious objections, including the Pope himself, spontaneously eulogized Sister Emmanuel's enthusiastic book. This favorable wind has spread to *La Croix* (April 7) and to *Le Monde* (April 28). Is it the war or the Gospa that alters the views of the media in such a way? How far will this movement go?

WAR: LOVE YOUR ENEMIES

5

FRUITS

The fruits from Medjugorje still come. Moreover, they spread and deepen with the hardships there and at the pilgrims' homes. Of course, superficial people fled away from Medjugorje when the war erupted. The message spoke of peace, and the contrary was happening. It was scandalous to some, but others reacted with depth.

1. IN MEDJUGORJE

In the village, the whirlwind of hotel and other trades that monopolized the overworked population during the years 1986-1991 had curbed massive involvement in the weekly mass, fasting and saying the rosary as a family. The parish had turned into a sort of secular monastery.

Like God's people in the Bible, hardship has brought many back. The example set by the visionaries (especially Vicka) and the Franciscans has brought a new kind of relief in the middle of the storm; recourse to the Holy Virgin and God is back.

The fighters, who protect the village against ethnic cleansing, rape and havoc, have their rosary and pray seriously. They are without hate as they face danger. They did not want to mobilize Ivan; they instead delegated him to more intense prayer. Despite being sent into the country's battlefield, these fighters recognize with gratitude that not one of them has yet died.

The visionaries who were dispersed, either to protect their family (Mirjana and Ivanka), or to escape mobilization by the Serbian-Yugoslavian army (Jakov) are slowly coming back to the village. From Vicka's example, they understand that it is their home. They lead perfectly honest lives. They live as good Christians and are, at different levels, sincere witnesses on their way to sainthood, which Vicka has attained in an exemplary manner.

They have given shelter to many refugees, notably more than a hundred children for Christmas; and they openly and generously manage the food relief and other needs that make their way to Medjugorje.

2. THE PILGRIMS

With courage and audacity, the pilgrimages, which had stopped due to the severity of the events and the danger, have started again; the pilgrims persevere in spite of the danger. An information capillary network indicates, at each phase of the fights, where and how one can get through.

After Jozo Zovko's appeal in May-June 1992, the pilgrimages have progressively begun again in many countries, bearing the same fruits of conversion, spiritual animation, and engagements which we will talk about later.

In France, the conspiracy to remain silent was particularly efficient so that she seemed one of the least sensible places about Medjugorje. Within the pilgrimage's multilingual enrollment (in Croatian, English, Italian, German) French was often omitted since it had few representatives.

France goes back to adversity

During the crisis, however, the French contingent has been particularly industrious. The Italian *Eco* remarked on the occasion of Christmas 1992:

-250 to 300 French speaking pilgrims! It is surprising since before the war they were not as present. But today they are very brave. They are the most numerous group. Then come the Americans, the Irish, the English and a small German group. There are also quite a few Italian - all together about 700 pilgrims from all parts of the world. They bring relief to the refugees who are in tremendous need.

We will see later the charitable and sometimes heroic dimension of these pilgrims.

Fourth youth festival

The youth festival, that has had so much success since its creation in 1990(DN 10, p. 76-79; DN 11, p. 65-67), in line with *l' Annee des jeunes* (DN 9, p. 178), has become an institution. It has been maintained in spite of the dissuasive circumstance of the war.

In 1992, it was officially renamed *"Rencontre internationale"* instead of *Festival*, but *Festival* continues to identify this event that was renewed for the third time from July 21 to August 6, the day of the Transfiguration. In spite of the war, a few hundred youth came from Italy, Austria, Germany and English speaking countries. Slavko guided this prayer meeting on the following theme (from one of Medjugorje's messages): *Come, see and decide for Peace.* The source of this appeal is faith and prayer because "who does not pray is dead, and humanity without spiritual nourishment is without life and is headed toward its irreparable ruin." He invited all to discern the signs God continually gives and to answer His call, while recognizing his own part in God's plan for Salvation. Ivan reminded the youth that by inviting them to reject the most profound sin of their heart, the Gospa brings joy. Marija and Vicka emphasized the importance of prayer and fasting, conversion, and mostly the mass. Jelena shared the experience of prayer in her group.

Tuesday, August 4, was a day of reflection and prayer in Slano, a village destroyed by the Serbs and which is located on the Dalmatian coast near Dubrovnik.

On Wednesday, August 5, the day when the visionaries discreetly celebrate The Holy Virgin's birthday (according to the confidence they received on its bimillenium in 1984), Father Jozo guided the prayers. He compared Medjugorje's pilgrims to Veronica, who brought comfort to Christ on the way to the Calvary. The leaders do not know how to stop the war. Only Mary do so through our praying and fasting. He related the story of an American officer in Medjugorje. By chance this career officer had met a pilgrimage of Croatian soldiers; and after a serious talk with them, he concluded:

You and I wear a uniform, but we are not identical because you wear the rosary around your neck. You have faith and you pray; but we, on the contrary, do not pray, and we place our faith in the strength of weapons. That is our mistake. I will resign from the functions of an officer to place myself at the service of the Church and of the Virgin Mary.

Father Jozo finished by stating:

Croatia will be the heel that will crush the venomous serpent that is Communism but that is also sin.

On the 5th, the youth were invited to Ivan's extraordinary apparition on the hill in Podbrdo. The Gospa invited them to pray for peace.

After the Transfiguration mass, Father Slavko dismissed the group by saying:

Go, and tell that you have seen - a country that suffers, believes and hopes (Echo 95, p. 4).

50

To guard against the difficulties of the trip, another Festival: *Jeunesse 2000* was celebrated in England in *Aylesford Priory*, Kent, from August 27 to 31, with Father Slavko, Ken Roberts and Elian Lawton (Echo 94, p.6).

One of the characteristics of the authentic work of Grace is that prayer and union with God develop from the inside resulting in efficient and brave actions. All of this had started a long time ago. The present drama and urgencies have amplified these fruits.

3. THE NEW COMMUNITIES

Communities stemming from Medjugorje continue to grow and to multiply.

On November 8 I again visited the Oasis community. Great plans to build on the virgin site acquired near Rome are being realized. During my visit in November 1992, two buildings were up, and others had been started. A prefabricated shack serves as a temporary chapel which is fervently visited.

The community continues with the same charisma and overcomes difficulties that are certainly present (DN 10 p. 72-75; DN 11. p.61-63).

On June 24, 1992, the new bishop of Vicenza (the diocese where the community had started in Priabona) definitely refused authorization to celebrate mass in the church they had acquired and remodeled. The community, rejected from the diocese, had discreetly kept this place where they would go to find themselves again. Without the use of the Church, it was impossible to continue. The bishop has cut the umbilical cord from its birth place. They are in exile, but the Oasis accepts it warm-heartedly. The journal of the same name announces the news with the headline, that is taken from Job's resigned adoration in Job 1, 21:

This church , *'The Lord gave, and the Lord has taken away; blessed be the name of the Lord!'*

The community visibly grows. (There were more than 70 members when I visited it , after 5 years of existence.) The foundations continue to multiply. At the end of 1991 a new community has been established in Pedara, Sicily.

In obedience to Monsignor Hnilica (the Slavic bishop who founded a community for testimonies to and evangelizing in Russia), Father Sgreva went to Moscow, on July 13, 1992 (anniversary of the message from Our Lady of Fatima on the end of the persecutions and the conversion of that country). He contacted the bishop named by John Paul II for the diaspora, which had been underground and outlawed for such a long time. The Vatican has been careful to name him as bishop *in* Moscow and not as bishop *of* Moscow, so as not to give umbrage to the Orthodox Patriarchate. Gianni Sgreva has thus met Monsignor Tadeusz Kondrusiewicz for the beginning of a community, not in Moscow but near the Volga so as not to hurt the Orthodox sensibility (*Revue Oasis* n. 10, Oct. 1992 p.3036).

Oasis' previous issue (June 25, 1992) celebrated another beginning, the highest, under the heading:

La Cummunaute Mariale de L'Oasis
has inaugurated his seat in Heaven

This article talks about the first deceased member of the community. Brother Antonello Maria died on Wednesday, March 11, 1992 at 9:00 p.m. He had had a terminal disease since November 20, 1989. He completely offered his life to Our Lady for the Community. During the days of his terminal disease, he wanted to put his hands and feet on the cross, like Christ, while asking the Holy Virgin to assure him of her help. On March 8 between 9:00 and 9:30 a.m., while still lucid, he asked to take his perpetual vows at this, the threshold of his painful extinction. Like a fertile seed, his death has had a profound effect on all.

Oasis has published his testament-letter dated February, 1989 in the October 1992 issue, p. 7-9. On this date, before learning of his fatal disease, he humbly asked forgiveness for his disobedience, because he had lived in ardent combat like Jacob, and he said these words that take on new meaning today:

I feel that I am on a way, now more than ever, a way of continuous conversion, with no stop in sight, no matter what the price. Maybe the highest vocation is to always renew oneself towards the Lord, the Eternal... towards God and His Love.

Each step represents a sign. Which step am I living today? (p.9).

Tomislav Vlasic

For the last three years, objectivity has forced us to give bad news on the community founded by Tomislav Vlasic. The importance he had given to the discussed visionary Agnes Heupel resulted in the emotional departure of Marija, Medjugorje's visionary; and most of those youth (a remarkably elite group) afterwards also left (DN 8, p.5054).

These failures and the resulting defamation made the canonical problem difficult. After this painful failure, what status should be given to a Medjugorjian community (whose apparition is still being discussed), founded by a Franciscan integrated by his vows to his religious community? We have never ceased to underline the admirable and faultless role that Tomislav Vlasic played from August 1981 to September 1984, a heroic time when he directed Medjugorje which was then under the double assault from the Communist government and the bishop of the area.

His calm and obedience to the laws of the Church and the state, his courtesy and especially the spiritual awakening he catalyzed in the parish and the pilgrimages, were more than providential; they were almost miraculous. He has kept his charisma. However some have wondered about his radical spiritual exigency: the love pushed to immolation. One wonders if this man, cheerfully superior to the plurality of heavy charges and the most severe adversities, is not like those ardent and powerful horses who best show their valor when they carry a heavy load, while their ardor would cause light cars to sway and turn over.

Tomislav Vlasic has deeply endured the challenge. He has maintained his stamina in spite of adversity. He continues to prove himself as a spiritual leader awakening and converting participants at the *Festival des jeunes* in Medjugorje and in Italy. He has again centered everything on the Gospel itself, saying that the apparitions' only role is to actualize. He has become one of the most influential spiritual personalities (if not the most influential) in Italy. He is the instigator, animator and reference to the 35 fraternities of souls given away without reserve, individuals throughout the peninsula who have been aroused by his predication.

He has finally found ecclesiastic status under the aegis of the Franciscan Order to which he belonged, not in Croatia, but in Italy. On November 14, 1991, *le Provincial des Freres Mineurs D'Abruzzo* gave him the green light to set up in his Province. Monsignor Antonio Valentini, Archbishop of Chieti, gave him oral authorization in December, 1992, then written, on January 15 to

> *form* l'Association privee de fideles Kraljice Mira (*Queen of Peace) established in the convent of the Franciscans of* Santa Maria della Misecordia, *in Lama Dei Peligni, located in the archdiocese of Pieti-Vasto* (Letter of May 20, 1992).

On May 20, 1992, le Provincial approved T. Vlasic's status and authorized

> *to continue* ad experimentum *this experience for 3 years of* Association privee de fideles, *under the direct responsibility of the Provincial Minister with all the rights and duties specified by the Canons 299, # 3 and 321-326 of the* Code de Droit Canon, *that govern these new private associations of faithful.*

That same day a letter from the Archbishop confirmed the foundation.

As he journeyed through the long dramatic tunnel between Parma (1988) and Chieti (1992), Tomislav progressively realized what had caused the failure of his first community.

Thus on June 25, 1992, the eleventh anniversary of the apparitions in Medjugorje, Tomislav, delegated by the Provincial (who was absent), presided over the ceremony of the first ten people, including Agnes, to take their final vows. (They wear a brown frock like the Franciscans.) Eleven other youth began their novitiate on the Feast of Saint Francis (October 4, 1992).

Four members of one of the first communities (the one in Parma - Danica, Senka, Ivanka, and Ignaz) persevered. This last square of Gideon's soldiers constitute a significant foundation. Among them, the Austrian Ignaz represents hope for the new foundation. He will soon be ordained a priest, along with Lino.

Moreover, 7 young girls and one Croatian boy are already the guests of the community, and are intensely preparing themselves to enter this demanding life.

Agnes Heupel, a sincere but much publicized member because of her visions and because of the considerable role that Tomislav gave to her in Parma (up to the point of com-

paring her to Saint Claire beside Saint Francis), occupies today a more modest place, more conforming to her grace. As
for Tomislav, he speaks little of the messages and refers more
and more to the Gospel and to its most radical requirements
according to Christ's words: "*The one who wants to come with
me must renounce himself, bear his cross and follow me.*" These
words and His example on the way to Calvary have inspired
in the Church, after the martyrs, the different victimized spiri-
tualities that have begun especially since the XVIIth century,
and that Paul Claudel immortalized in *L'Annonce faite a Marie.*

In the latest news, on May 20 Tomislav's community
started to move into the convent of S. Giovanni da Capestrano,
a convent that is being remodeled with a capacity for 40
people. On May 25, the first eleven youth finished their novitiate, and the six waiting Croatian replaced them. During a
retreat preached by Tomislav, 30 youth ready to follow these
often camp at the convent. They will enter when the remod-
eling is complete, in Autumn 1993.

While guiding this community within the framework of
the Franciscan convent, Tomislav is more and more often
called throughout Italy to lead the 35 fraternities inspired by
his predication and to preach the four annual retreats for them.

His spiritual influence is still growing without causing
any criticism. Some wonder, however, whether this man will
be able to awaken deep vocations, this watcher of God's future? Will he have the feel for the daily needs required to
form a community? Or will he find somebody to whom he
can delegate this work? Ignaz, for example?

A new and important fact is the support and cooperation
from the Franciscan Provincial of Abruzzo, who has felt the
spiritual quality of this project and contributed by obtaining
the bishop's approval and a convent worthy of this community.

The communities in Legnano (Milano) and Rome

Another prosperous community has been born from Medjugorje's inspiration, which today includes 161 members: 131 in Legnano, the others in Rome. Eleven sisters are getting ready for the consecration of the virgins, and 20 married members reside in Casa di Maria: *Gruppo giovanile dell'Accademia dell'Immacolata (Groupe de l'Academie de l'Immaculee)*, presided over by Cardinal Deskur. The two communities are led by an ardent, stable, and very discreet Milanese priest, 35-year-old Giacomo Martinelli. (He is in office with Cardinal Deskur.) The community is also lead by a 35-year-old theologian, prize winner of the Gregorienne.

On December 8, 1992, the Pope thanked them for leading the homage to the Holy Virgin in Espana court, around the column of the Immaculate Conception.

The community was officially approved under the name *Completamente tuoi* (Everything to you, according to Totus tuus of Monfort), by Cardinal Ruini, the Pope's vicar for the diocese in Rome, on January 30, 1993: 120 consecrated, 33 in la Casa di Maria in Rome (13 celibate, 20 married).

Reggio di Vernazza (Spezia)

A small community, also inspired by Medjugorje and led by total self-sacrifice, is growing near the sanctuary of Reggio di Vernazza (Spezia, Italy) around a hermit, Giovanni Bozzo. Families have joined the little group of youth who started it. Another house has been established to receive them (*Eco* 103, 3c).

Foggia

This community continues under a new form, after some vicissitudes and thanks to Oasis.

Scotland

The Eco (n. 100, p.8) brings attention to the birth of another Medjugorjian community in Scotland, citing the testimony of one of its members, Una Oliv:

For the last month (November, 1992), I have belonged to a youth community called Krizevac Youth Community in Dalmallly, and I am happy that the Holy Virgin called me here. This home of prayer follows Medjugorje's spirituality and the community of youth is at the service of prayer and evangelizing, under the direction of the Virgin Mary and her saintly messages. Pray for us and for all those who come to Craig Lodge, our Home.

4. THE PRAYER GROUPS

The hundreds of prayer groups continue, often over motivated by the actual drama and mobilized for charitable actions. In America, the centers that the *Queen of Peace* coordinates continue to multiply; there are almost 200 today.

In Medjugorje itself, all the groups we talked about continue with intensity, especially Ivan's group which gathers together on Monday night around 10:00 on the Hill of Apparitions, and on Friday on the Hill of the Cross - Krizevac. But there is a message only when Ivan is present.

5. CONFERENCES AND MEETINGS

The great American conferences, a list of which we gave up to September 1992, continue to occur with thousands of participants.

Conference Marian de Chicago, organized by Louis Malik, September 4-6,

Conference Marian, organized, also in Chicago, by
    Kathleen Long, October 2-4, 1992,
Marian Conference de Las Vegas (Nevada), November
    27-30, 1992,
Quatrieme Conference de L'Universite de Notre-Dame
    (Indiana), at Pentecost, May 29-30, 1993.

Great testimonies and prayer meetings are also added to
those. Father Slavko and Father Orec, along with one of the
visionaries (often Marija and/or Ivan, and more recently
Vicka), gather large crowds throughout many countries,
which is mentioned further in the chronology.

6. ECHOES AND RADIOS

Radio Maria has undergone a certain crisis. It has pushed
away its foremost contributors, such as Bonifacio, who sub-
sequently redirected himself by granting massive aid to
Hercegovina. This station, which has gained a very large audience, millions of listeners, lost its way in a polemic against
Vassula, who is so fervent towards the Holy Virgin and who
is slandered with an iconoclast relentlessness that does not
favor the peace Our Lady inspires. Many pray so that these
strange temptations be overcome by the fervent priest who
leads this bright private chain.

The subsidiaries of *Radio Maria* continue to multiply and
to develop, especially in Poland (DN 11, p.64). Their set up
escaped a great fire around the town of Torun, where their
station is located.

In this calamity, we have all prayed non-stop for rain to
come, ultimate savior and... the rain came, in the night of
August 7-8. In Torun, 200 000 people were saved. The fire
was rapidly getting close to the military depots. If it had
reached them, it would have been a catastrophe. [...] At a
time when the enemies of the Church attack and spread er-

ror, Mary is with us and always finds new collaborators. Our people are not yet spoiled by all that comes from the West. In our turn, we work at saving and helping the West through numerous disciples of Christ educated at the school of Mary by this radio.

Radio Maria of Poland celebrated its first anniversary on December 8, the Feast of the Immaculate Conception. It is gaining support from the bishops, including Cardinal Glemp. They dreamt of a satellite link that would allow the radio to broadcast to all of the dioceses. It is now done: on February 27, 1993, Cardinal Glemp convened in Warsaw with the director of *Radio Maria* to increase its audience "to millions of Catholics from his diocese and from all others." *Radio Maria* broadcasts with a 198 meter antenna on the ex-palace of the Culture of Warsaw. There is a total of 33 stations. The gifts that came from Italy allowed this great accomplishment. Sister Margherita Makarovic was its support by her sacrifice. She sent word to Father Tadeusz before her death: "*I offer everything for Radio Maria*" (Eco 102, p.7).

7. SOCIAL DIMENSION

Medjugorje for the children

Medjugorje, which is sometimes accused of being a mystical evasion, is no stranger to society's poverty. Mauro Harsch, professor at the Conservatory of Music of Lugano, continues the edification and meeting of the *Centres d'accueil* which he founded, with the help of Medjugorje's friends, for the orphans of Bombay and Brazil (DN 11, p. 67). (Another welcoming center for Croatian orphans is under consideration in Medjugorje. It will start when the war is over.)

In Brazil, the Centers welcome children who are wild, anti-social, without family and who wander about the city-jungles of Sao Paulo and Rio. Otherwise many are shot like rabbits or kidnapped for their organs - methods used to dispose of them.

Sister Elvira and the regeneration of drug addicts

Sister Elvira's communities thrive. They work with a seemingly hopeless disease, drug addiction. In the last 9 years, Sister Elvira has founded 17 Communities, with one in Medjugorje and one in Split.

The houses are managed by the ex-addicts themselves. They are young seculars who do not take any vows, but their life is demanding. Everyday they must spend three hours in prayer, and no television.

Contact with Vicka has brought a lot to Medjugorje's Community. For a long time camping was necessary, but a real house has now been built next to Vicka's.

Under the tents, the heat was unbearable, Sister Elvira tells. But Providence was there combined with intuition, good will, hard work, and perseverance from these youth. In order to build their house without any mechanical means, they cut large rocks with chisels, hammers, and sledgehammers. In six to seven months, they finished their work with the consciousness of also building lost interior values. They persevered with constancy even while tired from working hard. [...]. Today, we can even accommodate you. [...] I remain in a state of wonder. (Echo, n. 95).

Stephane, one of the boys from the Community, testifies:

The world will change when we will know how to offer, to give Jesus Christ to the young . [...] Nothing else can assuage the nostalgia and the thirst for the absolute that is in a young person's heart. And I guarantee you that the heart of an addict desires (more than anything else) *freedom, the azure sky and the infinite! He aspires to these with such an intensity that he is willing to go to the depths of hell thinking he will find good. . . . Jesus-Christ is found in silence. I think that young people are afraid of silence. Yesterday, a young boy came here to Medjugorje and ran away two hours later. The silence that resides here, where so many people pray to the Holy Virgin, un-settled him. Rather than showing himself as a pauper, a loser (even he if did not use drugs)... he chose to run away. God does not resist anybody, but He cannot do anything for the proud ones. He cannot give anything to those with a closed heart. Thus, I hope from the bottom of my heart that all of us, each evening, feel like losers who have many good resolutions but who accomplish few of them; because we must have a need for God and our people more than the air we breathe.*

The Gospel this morning (Lk 10, 38-41) made me think: Martha welcomes Jesus into her home. Mary sits at His feet, and welcomes Him into her heart. It is not enough to welcome Jesus and Mary (who has been here for more than eleven years) into the house, *into the prayer group, into the parish, if we do not welcome Him* into our heart *as a personal and radical choice of our life. Even in a community, each one of us must welcome Jesus into his heart. It is God's mystery that leaves man free. If we welcome Jesus into our heart by an act of will, if we want to meet Jesus Christ and Mary, they will come to us. This is God's love. Me, I would not change the life I am living for millions, even if so many times I go to bed exhausted, even if it feels heavy at times, even if I cry sometimes, I scream. No, I will not change, even for mil-lions!*

I would not change the love we live in the Commu-nity for any other human love; neither would I change

*the affection that I personally devote to Elvira. This is
an attachment that goes beyond humanity. The love Elvira
devotes to us is not limited to human love, but it comes
from the heart. Elvira loves us with God's love, a love
that engenders life, harmony, and joy in us.*

*If our love is not born out of prayer, then I think it is
a little false, because it is full of hidden ambitions. Charity is humility, liberty and silence, which prayer teaches
us. Without prayer, even the good we do for others remains barren, because it does not spring back up onto
us. Near here, the Madonna has been coming everyday
for the last eleven years; that is because it is a serious
matter. Otherwise, She would not have come here everyday to tell us: 'Wake up, change your life!'*

*If it were not a matter of something grand and beau-
tiful, Mary would not have come here for such a long
time. In Fatima and in Lourdes, she stayed a little while;
but think about how she changed things. [...] If it were
not to prepare something grand, She would have not come
here! We must take Her seriously.* (Testimony received
by A. Bonifacio, July 1992, *Echo 95*).

When we read this ex-addict's testimony and so many
others, when we see these radical life changes, we wonder
how Medjugorje's adversaries can attribute all these graces to
a "trick of the devil" - how these honest Christians do not see
the devil elsewhere in their polemic.

English doctors, amazed by such rapid and perfect detoxi-
fication, have asked for information about the therapeutic
method used by this Sister. Sister Elvira, a stranger to any
kind of laboratory and technical study, tried to answer, but in
a style that discouraged these scientific thinkers:

Everything happens in the warm and truly saintly
Chapel we call the Chamber of Miracles. Every day

the young men experience there the deep therapy they need from that unique and irreplaceable Therapist. Not only does He heal the wounds, but He also make them shine. We are becoming prophets of Hope. If prayer is profound, true and vital, we cannot leave the Chapel the same way we entered it. It would really be wasting our life. It is the place where Jesus remains, waiting for us day and night. And it is the place where each day starts, after the wake up call, usually around 6 o'clock. We get together in the Chapel; we say the rosary that puts us under the Holy Virgin's protection. Only She can lead us to purity, through Jesus's love. Here, so many young people have again found, besides healing, the joy of life and testimony.

The Holy Spirit has forced me to open my eyes to the most abandoned and betrayed young - especially drug-dependent youth. Thus our community was born in 1983 on the hill of Saluzzo (in the province of Cuneo). The cenacle started in a house the town gave us, an abandoned building that was falling apart. We just got to work. We opened our hearts to God, and He did not make us wait. Our community was born out of Providence.

For the last 9 years, we live this life experience each day, and we are happy to be able to say that anyone who confides in God is never disappointed.

Since then, 17 other houses have been given to the community in order that this infallible and radical cure can grow. We have always been patient, sleeves up, praying fervently and constantly, working hard. We have always refused any economic aid that any public institution may offer because we stake our faith in God. This is not utopia. God really makes the water spurt out of the rock. Providence does not happen

without suffering. That's why, when we do not have something, we do without and wait until faith overcomes this obstacle through prayer. What we offer to these young drug-
dependents is the rebirth that goes through the cross - yes,
the cross, welcomed, accepted and loved. She leads to Resurrection, Truth and Life.

These youth learn the Ave Maria communally; they learn
to kneel in the weakness itself that had been their downfall.
They are thus learning Christian life - the life of Christ.

*Not to deceive them, we propose the concrete truth of
God's Words and mean to practice these like they are,
without reducing them or imposing them by force. (Echo
98, p. 7b).*

Sister Elvira was in Lourdes with Vicka on November 28-
29. She was looking for a way to open a house to receive drug
addicts in Lourdes or its surroundings. She recently sent three
young people to Florida to found a new community.

Mother Theresa asked her to found a community in
Calcutta. She will help.

Prayer in jails

Prayer in jails continues (LN 10, LN 11). Vassula never
fails to visit them during her trips to the USA.

In the prison at Delmont, New Jersey, fifty year old James
Krowl, has been serving, since May 1988, a 10 year sentence
for armed robbery. He has kept a journal of his daily Rosary
since January 1989 and writes about conversions and healing, as well as visitors: Father Gianni Sgreva, founder of *Oasis* in Rome, and Dom Stefano Gobbi. Mr. Krowl gives thanks
to God, especially for the healing of his son who had been
suffering from AIDS. However, he tells us that the greatest
blessing that he has been given in returning to God and Ca-

tholicism is love. "I can now honestly say that I know Love. I can love my brothers and even those I would not have loved spontaneously. "

I have thus received, through Maureen Dean's intermediary, information concerning the leader of the prayer group in the prison at Delmont. He had abandoned the Church in 1959. That same year he was arrested as a runaway, then convicted for kidnapping and other crimes. He returned to the Catholic Church on October 17, 1980. Monsignor Toomey heard his confession for a long time in the prison at Trenton. James received the Eucharist, joined Dom Gobbi's movement, and prayed the consecration to God through Mary according to Grignion de Monfort in December 1990. After joining the prison's Rosary group in April 1990, he became the group leader in June of the same year. The group prays together daily.

Aid to the war victims

Medjugorje's message has mobilized generous, efficient and sometimes heroic aid, in spite of bomb attacks and their threat.

France is in a good place for this mobilization. Initiatives are multiplying. Among a few are

-   Florence de Gardelle who regularly conveys 24 ton trucks;
-   Arlette Sonnet, from Lyon;
-   Paul Imbert and Blandine (his daughter), from Clermont-Ferrand;
-   From France, near Ars, Regis Clauz who distributes relief directly through the pilgrims: 108 tons in 1992, 160 in 1993;
-   Francois Bray, from Tours;
-   the Hallos, from Rouen;
-   Michel Poste; etc.

Genevieve Bastard makes this appeal through her *Association Notre-Dame de la Paix* (19, rue du Jour, 75001 Paris):

1. Our goal is one pilgrimage per month.
2. We are collecting non-perishable food. We also receive gifts by check paid to the order of SOS Medjugorje, addressed to the Association Notre-Dame de la Paix. Those we have already received have allowed us to buy wholesale at good prices. That is how the last 25 ton trucks left on July 24. Upon our arrival, we witnessed the refugees' joy, those who have lost everything: their house, their future, and maybe their homeland. We are still looking for more trucks and drivers.

The biggest help probably comes from Italy. Alberto Bonifacio, a young retired man, dedicates his whole life to this work with Chiarina Daolio. They assure, alternately or together, two relief convoys of about thirty trucks each, twice a month. At the beginning of 1992, a convoy of 82 trucks each containing 10 tons of food left Vicenza. The group *Soppelsa-Cabrini* has sent 500 trucks plus monetary contributions (Medjugorje, Genova, February 1993, p. 32)

Each month for several months England has sent ten trucks, and she has also contributed 15 ambulances.

Austria has sent 50 tons of flour and 50,000 Marks. The money often comes from door-to-door collecting.

Even Africans from Malawi have sent winter clothes.

Help also comes from the adoption, by the thousands, of orphans of the ethnic war and children born from rapes committed by the Serbs (*supra*, p. 39).

When those who bring help to Hercegovina are thanked, they often answer:

-We should thank you. We have received so much from Medjugorje! It is there we have started a new life. We are free of all sorts of poisons (Echo 99. p. 4-5)...

A Serb-Croatian Home

We should mention a testimony that is, at the same time, a reality and a symbol. Sabrina Covic, a Croatian very dedicated to Medjugorje, produced , in August 1992, a very beautiful video: *Medjugorje MIR*, distributed by Sakramento, BP 85, 93141, Bondy Cedex. She married a Serb, and this marriage has for them a special meaning in the wake of Medjugorje's reconciliatory message.

I am a Croatian from Osijek near Vudokar; in the midst of the Serb-Croatian war, on November 23, 1992, we got married at Noisy-le-Sec, a Parisian suburb.

Vladan Radojicic (my husband) and I love and respect each other very much. The national problems are very difficult to handle , but we do everything possible to show that something else can exist besides hate.

I am a Medjugorje fanatic, and I feel each one of Mary's words as being directly addressed to me. I know I have my role to play in the reconciliation.

The actual human experiences are perfectly demonic. I did not believe in the devil before, but now I strongly believe in him. When you are a man, you do not kill a small child just for pleasure - nor anybody else either for that matter...

I am leaving for Belgrade on November 28, 1992, and I will see if there are prayer groups over there with which we can collaborate. We wish to help from here by organizing intertwined prayers from the perspective of the Marian message of reconciliation. As far as I know, it has not been done yet.

At this moment, I am alone in this. It is still a private initiative that might bear fruit someday.

Mary had a purpose when she united my husband and myself.

Fewer than 30 % of the Serbs are baptized. Those are the official numbers. These people have no catechism, and they are very far away from God. They search for God because they are thirsty, but they do not know the God of love who is ours. More and more often, they say that God is just energy.

How can you expect a people who say that God is only energy to give value to a human being? Human beings are nothing then! An entire generation will be destroyed in Serbia because they are so far from God. When they hear the word "Catholic", it is as if they heard "Devil", because they are sure that we Catholics only want to baptize them as Catholic... the newspapers tell them this.

They do not know that the God of the Orthodox and the God of the Catholics are the same; only the rites are different. Moreover, they do not know that we are not baptized as Catholics, but as Christians, that is in the Name of the Father and of the Son and of the Holy Spirit... all of us.

From all my heart, as a Catholic and as a child of Mary, I must try to help them. They are on their way to perdition.

– Sabrina Covic

In the Bible, there are some symbolic marriages: God invites the prophet Hosea to marry a prostitute. The meaning of this live parable shows His desire to reconcile with His adulterous people. He wants to take her back as a "fiancee" without sin (Hosea 2, 21 and Cant. 4, 7). But the symbolism mentioned above is different from the reconciliation between

Serbs and Croatians that Sabrina and Vladan want to represent. They deliberately radiate, in Medjugorje and elsewhere, their beautiful message of peace, that hide, but also bear, other Serb-Croatian couples.

Healing

News circulates (circumstances not permitting serious inquiry) that healing continues to occur. Slavko pointed to two of them which occurred during the Summer of 1992.

In August, a French lady who had several surgeries on her leg went up to Podrdo on her crutches to pray in the evening, with Ivan's group. At the time of the apparition, she felt a heat diffuse throughout her whole body as her leg came back to life. Joyously she went back down without her crutches.

On September 13, the same thing happened to an American woman approaching 60, condemned to a wheelchair. After the blessing for the sick given by Father Jozo in Siroki Brijeg, she got up from her wheelchair; stunned by the unforeseen healing, she thanked the Gospa. (Eco 96, p. 3a, that does not give any names and leaves hope for specifications).

Slavko specified that the name of the American woman is Nancy Lauer.

I met her on the day of the celebration of the Exaltation of the Holy Cross (September 14, 1992), in front of the parish church. I thought I had seen, a few days earlier, this person walking on crutches... The truth is, I was not sure of it. Thus I questioned her.

S. - Who are you and where do you come from?

N. - *My name is Nancy Lauer. I am American. I am 55 years old and the mother of 5 children. Until now, my life has only been a life of suffering. Since 1973, I have been from hospital to hospital. I have had numerous serious surgeries: one on my neck, one on my spine, and two on my hips. My whole body has always been in pain, and my left leg was shorter than my right leg. In the last two years, a swelling has appeared in my left kidney, giving me a great deal of pain. I had a difficult childhood. As a child, I was raped. This left an incurable wound which contributed to the failure of my marriage. My children have suffered much from it. On the other hand, I must shamefully confess that because of these tremendous familial problems for which I could not find a solution, I slowly turned to alcohol. However, recently, I have been able to recover.*

S. - In such a situation, how did you decide to come to Medjugorje?

N. - *An American community was preparing a pilgrimage, and I had the ardent desire to participate. My family tried to dissuade me with solid arguments, so I did not insist. But at the last moment, a pilgrim changed his mind; and with the OK from my family, I took his place. Something was irresistibly attracting me here... and now, after 9 years of infirmity, I walk without crutches. I am healed.*

S. - How did the healing occur?

N. - *In September 1992, just before the beginning of the Rosary [around 6:00 p.m.], I went up with the other group members to the church tribune. We prayed. At the end, when Ivan the visionary kneeled and started to pray, I felt a very strong pain throughout my body. It is with great effort that I did not scream. Whatever happened, the Holy Virgin was there. I was making an effort to be aware of her presence. I did not even realize that the apparition was over and that Ivan had gotten up. At the end, we were told to descend from the tribune. I wanted to take my crutches, but surprisingly, I felt a new force in my legs. By habit I took hold of the crutches, but I got up with an incredible easiness. When I started to walk, I understood I could do it without any support and without any help. I went slowly towards the house where I resided. I went up and down my bedroom without any effort. Moreover, I started jumping and dancing... It was incredible! It was a new life!*

I forgot to tell you that at the time of the healing, I stopped limping because of this shorter leg. I could not believe it myself; so I asked a friend to watch me while I walked. She confirmed that I was not limping anymore. Finally, the swelling around my left kidney has also disappeared.

S. - How did you pray then?

N. - I said: "Mary, I know You love me and I too love You. Help me to do God's will. Me, I have the strength to handle my infirmity, but You, help me to always follow God's will." I did not know yet I was going to be healed, and I was still in pain. But I was already in a perfect state of love towards God and the Holy Virgin... and I was ready to endure my condition.

S. - Now, how do you see your future?

N. - Before anything else, I will dedicate myself to pray-
ing. But my duty will also be to testify to the merciful
love that God has for us. I am convinced that this miracle
will help my family to convert, to come back to prayer
and to live in peace (Interview by Slavko Barbaric, in
Nasa Ognista, translated in *Eco* 98, p. 4; and abstracted
in *Stella Maris* N. 280, p. 15).

The Italian *Eco* mentions the interior healing of a couple
from Padua, who testify:

I must insist today as in the past, God is a healer. He is
the remedy, as Saint Leopold said. He heals better than
psychotherapists. How many times had I thought about
that science, but God knows our depths. When we offer
ourselves and totally sacrifice ourselves, He manifests
Himself; He lights up the dark. We discovered the roots
of our hurt during the spiritual exercises preached by
Father Tomislav. God welcomed us like sons. He held us
close to His heart. He has forgiven us. He has bathed us
in liberating, redeeming and sanctifying grace, that is
stronger than any scientific proof. We will testify about
our healing.

Golden legend?

On top of those, Sister Emmanuel and Eco have added
other disconcerting facts.

Our friend Josip's family, 6 people total, has welcomed
12 refugees who have lost everything. Before the war,
Josip had killed a cow and was able to preserve the meat
in a freezer, working with a generator because the elec-
tricity had long been cut off since May-June 1992.

The family generously opens their table at all times to the poor - 18 people at lunch and dinner, without counting those who pass by. They are the only ones who can do it, because Providence allows them keep their generator working unlike those in the other houses. " We still have our house, our cattle and our fields. The others have nothing," they say.

The other evening, I asked Josip:

- Where have you been getting your meat at lunch and dinner for more than a month? Did someone give you another cow?

-No, Sister, it is still the same one, Josip answered. *I don't understand. I keep taking pieces from the freezer. and they never diminish. I even give some to other families.*

Providence cannot resist those hearts, Sister Emmanuel comments. *I thank God for the beautiful signs of His tenderness in the heart of Medjugorje, submerged in this never ending horror.* (Eco 94, p. 49).

She further tells:

A man in Medjugorje was very poor; because of the war, he had hardly anything to eat, only a few kilos of potatoes. Then refugees arrived, even poorer than he. He decided to welcome them into his home and to give them the few potatoes he had. Seeing his generous heart, other refugees came to ask him for some. After 3 days, his meager stack should have disappeared. But no! Not only had it not disappeared, but also the more he gave his potatoes, the bigger his stack became! Thanks to this, he was able to feed many poor. He found himself before 530 kilos of potatoes!

The same miracle occurred for the few beans he distributed freely. He was so moved by this gift from God that he was crying while telling us the story. I am reminded of a word from the Gospa:
-With love, my dear children, you will do what seems impossible (E 109).

Sister Emmanuel compares these unbelievable stories to similar experiences that were her own in the *Beatitudes spiritual family*.

Since I have joined a community, I have had several occasions to see with my own eyes the multiplication of food. The Lord multiplied by the thousands [during a meeting in Ars], chicken legs, bread loafs and chocolate.
"Prayer from the heart is all powerful", the Gospa said. This admirable family had started by giving freely and without knowing from where the solution to their need would come.

Other signs

Many who have lived in these heroic times have a sense of the miraculous throughout the hardships. One obvious example is the pilot ordered but unable to bomb St. James Church in Medjugorje. He could not see his target despite its being obviously visible from a plane.

Another coincidence discussed in Croatia concerns a train, without a conductor, that the Serbs had directed toward the Croatian port of Zara. It was supposed to explode in the chemical plants of the town. The damages would have been catastrophic, but the train derailed in a tunnel about 15 km from the town (*Echo* 101, p. 5bc).

Although there were attempts to intimidate Medjugorje at the beginning of May, she is, as of this writing, no longer threatened. The Serbs have installed a firing field behind apparition hill and have mobilized men from the village to keep a permanent look out on the other side. They are still there at the time I write.

The Spanish Blue Helmets, in charge of protecting humanitarian relief to Bosnia, have chosen this oasis of peace to establish 200 soldiers and their modern tanks. They actually have found vast amounts of room in the bungalows constructed for the pilgrims. They have been there for six months, from November 4, 1992 until May 4, 1993. Is that why the Pope told the Franciscan General:

-Isn't it a miracle that nothing was destroyed in Medjugorje?

Father Slavko told Sister Emmanuel about another source of surprising protection:

One of my friends from Medjugorje was sent with a dozen other soldiers into a very dangerous zone near the plain of Medjugorje, near the Neretva; the Serb planes started firing all over this zone. For hours they endured a rain of fragmentary bombs (outlawed by the Geneva Convention). Once the storm was over, they realized that the whole plain was burned. There were holes everywhere - except for the few square meters they were on. These men then understood that they had benefited from an unimaginable protection, and they promise God to never blaspheme again (blaspheming being an unfortunate habit among the Croatians).

At the time I write, none of the men from Medjugorje have been killed, and they have been mobilized since the beginning of the war in Hercegovina and have often been sent to hot spots, Mostar in particular. It is the only village without casualties. (I met soldiers from Siroki Brijeg. From the same number of men as that of Medjugorje, they had had thirty casualties.)

The Moslems had voted for independence along with the Croatians. The Croatians welcomed and fed their refugees and even gave them arms to defend themselves against the Serbs' sordid attacks. But lately we have observed in the airports the circulation of Moudjahijins, who have come to counsel, arm, and train the Moslems for total war. Since the beginning of May 1993, "ethnic cleansing" has been their agenda, especially in Kuljic and Jablanca. The Croatians had welcomed 180,000 Moslems, chased by the Serbs, into Croatian territory. Having become the majority, the Moslems in turn, applied the Serbs' tactics against the Croatians - attacks, pillages and massacres. In Kroujic, they started with the Franciscan convent, in spite of the fact the latter distrib uted relief equitably from the Catholic *Caritas* to Moslems as well as Croatians. Even in Mostar, contrary to what the international press says, it is not the Croatians but the Moslems who first attacked the Croatian's arm depots of which they were aware having used them before. The Croatians retaliated, and the conflict in that town appears to have no solution.

This new situation has created extreme confusion and discouragement. Under these conditions, what will happen to the mobilized soldiers in Medjugorje, of which none had been killed or hurt until now? In May 1993, they had their first wounded in Mostar, while many died in the close-by Croatian villages Citluk and Ljubuski. The horizon has become very dark. The Holy Virgin redoubles her plea for prayer.

Considering the information printed by the press, which is biased in favor of the Moslems and which attributes the offensive initiative to the Croatians, I have been surprised by but understand Mirjana's peaceful but bitter reflections on this sad reversal. Despite all, she perseveres in saying:

> *Let's pray, let's not judge, let's not hate, let's pray. As a Croatian, I have first suffered from Communism, then the war. I was taught that whoever wears his cross on earth will go to paradise, and without the cross we cannot go to paradise. Thus, we Croatians, are a people chosen by God to bear the cross and help Him, first with the Serbs and today with the Moslems [...] who now are also killing us [...]. We feel loved by God. I pray for the end of hate. If it is easy to talk when one has not lost anything, it is different when one loses family, house, country, everything. We must especially pray for the small children who have committed no sins (Echo 102, p. 6-1).*

Love for the enemy

The facts told in this chapter will often call for verification. But the most incredible fruit in Medjugorje, besides the generous help in this time of danger, is the love shown for the enemy. The visionaries, the Franciscans and those who listen to them live and shine love.

This represents God and the Gospel's unimpeachable signature.

6

TESTIMONIES

Although not as numerous because of the small number of pilgrims, conversions are still occurring in Medjugorje. Most of them remain a secret of the confessional, but a few of them have filtered through.

The wisdom of 70 "madmen"

During the slow times of Spring 1992, when the civil war in Bosnia Hercegovina started, the most important pilgrimage, precursor of those that started in June, was the one of the 70 "madmen" who left New England and California for Medjugorje. "A suicidal trip!" They were told.

They left against all odds. The war was one more motive for a praying pilgrimage to Our Lady of Peace. It took them three days to go from New York to Vienna, and 18 hours by car from Zagreb to Markarska on the Adriatic coast. They went to Medjugorje everyday, bringing bread and water so as not to deprive the refugees for whom they had each brought a relief suitcase.

In that particularly tragic month of May, when the visionaries, the Fathers and the population felt "abandoned by the Americans", this group of pilgrims was welcomed with joy. The Church was reopened for them, and they did not hesitate to pray on the two hills, despite the warning that the Serbs would fire on anybody (Echo p.94, p. 5)

Belgian Challenge

In Autumn of 1992, Pierre-Jean Haunecart, born in the south of France, left Belgium where he resides and did the pilgrimage on foot: almost 3,000 km both ways. He told Father Slavko:

> *Why did I do this pilgrimage? I cannot find a really satisfying response in myself. Simply, something moved me and I took to the road. It is my third pilgrimage, after Saint-Jacques de Compostelle and Assise. It is upon coming back from Assise last Spring (1991), during a stop in a minuscule church, that I found a small publication on Medjugorje. I had no idea what it was about, and I do not speak Italian. However my heart turned towards this unknown place. Afterwards, I learned about the facts and I came. Because of the terrible war, my pilgrimage for Christmas became a pilgrimage for peace [...]. A true pilgrimage is certainly not an adventure, nor a research for signs and miracles. A pilgrimage is to let oneself be moved by the search for God.*
>
> *I came here, focusing on the essential. I mostly prayed for peace and for your beautiful earth which is today bathed in blood. I prayed for the Croatian people, that they learn everything they must from this suffering. I prayed for your enemies, that they become aware of the evil they commit and that they change their behavi or by coming back to that which is essential - God.* (Echo 96, p.6)

Chinese in Medjugorje

At the end of July 1991, a group of Chinese made a pilgrimage to Medjugorje's Church.

> -*The messages have reached many Chinese towns, where prayer groups developed*, they said.

They had received the journal *Echo* in English and had read many translated articles in Chinese by Antony Tsoi.

One of these articles tells the story of Chang, who consecrated his life to the Holy Virgin. In 1988 one of his family members became gravely ill. Chang prayed for his recovery. That was the beginning of a conversion. A Trappist Father told him about Medjugorje. He read the messages and changed his whole life. He asked forgiveness for his past because there had been a long gap since his consecration at 15 - 40 years of a deviant life.

> *From that moment on,* he himself said, *I only desired one thing: to pray deeply and to give myself to divine Providence.*

With the help of a Monk, he organized prayer meetings. In Hong-Kong, he founded the first groups which are now multiplying. So many people come that they have to clear the ping-pong table, one of the most important things in China. A Protestant came to join the prayer group, but he was unsympathetic with the Rosary. Chang asked him:

> -You respect my mother, your mother, and all of your friends' mothers?
> -*Certainly*, he answered.
> -*Well*, Chang said, *the Holy Virgin is the Mother of Jesus, the Mother of us all.*

Chang helps the homeless. Lately, a young colleague who was terminally ill decided to be baptized, on the day of his death. A lady who had breast cancer completely offered her suffering and became a convert after the success of her surgery.

> -*By worshipping a lot, I save a lot of time*, he said.

Chang went on his first pilgrimage to Medjugorje in 1989; his second was in July 1991.

A provocative star becomes the star of Notre-Dame

On January 17, 1993, at a prayer meeting organized by Dr. Mansour in Los Angeles, California, I met Lola Falana, whose testimony I had already related (LN 11). I had not realized that she was one of the most famous singer-dancer-actresses in the USA: "the first lady of Las Vegas". She was also one of the most provocative.

Her conversion was no joke. She has completely changed her life - no more music-hall numbers. Her dress, always elegant, artistic even, has become modest. She lives alone, and for God only. With her generous temperament, she militates for great causes - especially to save the lives of the unborn threatened by abortion. For this cause, she fasted until she was given a television show to deliver her message. At Dr. Mansour's convention, she brightly testified of her conversion to God and Our Lady. She keeps in incredible contact with her audience. Even though her gestures are perfectly natural, they are so expressive that one would think they were studied and repeated with the same professionalism that she had for her sexy shows of the past. But she does not show her body anymore; she speaks through her eyes and gestures.

-I do not want to just be a tool used to attract people to my heavenly family, she says.

Her number one dialogue is with God. She tells Him:

Your name is I AM, and I belong to You with all that I am. That is what liberated me. Before, I would say, 'I think, I wish and I hope.' Now I am healed. All that I am comes from God. Once and for all, I have given Him my thoughts, my heart, my soul and my mind. Once and for all, I have given Him all that I am. [...] Now, I have no power without Him. Everything must come from my Manager, my Agent: Jesus-Christ. In the show business, everyone knows that you cannot succeed without somebody knowledgeable, without a contact. I had to learn that I am nothing. All of my gifts come from God, and they will not work to their full potential unless they are at the service of the Creator.

This transparency makes her shine.

She was born during the war, but still looks like a lively and radiant young girl. She has lost many of her old friends, but does not regret it. She wants to live for Jesus only; and, through Him, other friends come.

She reads Theresa of Avila and Saint John of the Cross, researching union with God. She already lives it so much and in such a sensible manner that I asked her:

-So do you have locutions or apparitions?
-*Neither*, she answered me, *but He inspires me and gives me proofs.*

WAR: LOVE YOUR ENEMIES

7

MESSAGES

Again we record Our Lady's messages from where we left off in LN 11, May 12, 1992.

We are surprised that Our Lady is not front page news with regards to the war and our future. She is not everyday news because she has another purpose. She programs solutions in depth by recommending praying, fasting, resistance to the devil's traps and the gift of oneself. She knows that the rest will follow. Thus here are the messages, which do not attract the merely curious, but those who wish to live life fully.

May 25:

Today again, I call on you for prayer. It is through prayer that you will come closer to God. I am with you, and I want to lead you on the way to the Salvation Jesus gives you. From day to day, I am closer to you, even if you are not aware of it and do not want to see it because you are only tied to me a little, with so little prayer. When tests or problems occur, you say: "Oh God, Oh Mother! Where are you?" And I only wait for the gift of your yes, to present it to Jesus, so that He can accord you His grace.

That is why, one more time, accept my call and start to pray anew, until prayer becomes joy for you. Then you will discover that God is almighty in your everyday life.

I am with you and I await you.

June 24, to Ivan, on Mount Krizevac, at the occasion of the 11th anniversary:

Thank Jesus Christ! I bring you peace. Bring it to others. You are those who will bring peace to the world.

June 25, to Ivanka, for her 7th annual apparition, the Holy Virgin had held out her hand as if to extend the gift of peace onto the people gathered in her house. Ivanka grasped her hands. The Gospa became very solemn, Ivanka specified:

Intensify prayer to defend yourself against Satan who wants to destroy you as well as the peace in your heart.

June 25, to Marija:

Now, I am happy, even if in my heart there is still some sadness for all of those who started on the right way and abandoned it.

The purpose of my presence is to lead you on a new way - the way to Salvation. That is why I ask you day after day for conversion. But if you do not pray, you cannot say you are on your way to conversion.

I pray for you and I intercede with God for peace - first for peace in your heart, and then for peace around you, so that God becomes your peace.

She gave a special benediction for that anniversary day.

June 29, Monday, to Ivan on the hill of Podbrdo:

Tonight, I especially invite you to abandon yourself to me. Unload all your problems and difficulties. I mostly ask you to start living the messages again. Pray now. I need your prayer!

July 25, to Marija:

Again today, I invite you all to pray, a prayer of joy. In these sad days, leave all your sadness in prayer and be in a joyous union with God your Creator.

Pray, little children, to be closer to me and to feel, through prayer, what I desire from you.

I am with you, and everyday I bless you with my benediction as a Mother so that the Lord will bless you all with the abundance of His grace in your everyday life.

Thank God who gives me the power to be with you because, I am telling you, it is a great grace!

August 3, Monday, to Ivan, on the hill of Podbrdo:
Dear children, I call on you to preserve peace in prayer.

August 14, Friday, on Mount Krizevac:
Dear children, now I ask you to say the Rosary in your family; pray more. Offer the Rosary for peace.

August 25, to Marija:
Dear children, I love you; today I want you to know it. I love you with all my love as a Mother; and I invite you to open up to me so that with each one of you, I can convert and save this world where there are so many sins and such evil.

That is why, my dear little children, completely open yourself to me, so that I can always lead you towards the wonderful love of God the Creator, who reveals Himself to you day by day.

I am with you, and I desire to reveal you and to show you the God Who loves you.

September 4, Friday, to Ivan, on Mount Krizevac:
Today again especially, I invite you to pray for peace. I need your prayers. Thank you, dear children, for answering my call.

September 12, Saturday, the eve of the Day of the Cross, to Ivan, on Mount Krizevac:
Dear children, I ask you to persevere in your prayer for peace.

September 25, to Marija:
Today again, I want to tell you that I am with you in these terrible days during which Satan wants to destroy what I and

my Son are building. He especially wants to destroy your souls. He wants to take you away as far as possible from Christian life as well as from the vital commandments of the Church. Satan wants to destroy all that is saintly in you and around you.

That is why, little children, pray, pray , pray to be able to seize all that God gives you through my visits.

October 2, Friday, to Ivan, on Mount Krizevac:

Again tonight your Mother addresses you with her very special call for prayer now, because right now Satan is trying to act through little things, dear children. That is why you must pray now! Satan is strong and he wants to make you deviate from your ways in order to destroy my plan for peace.

October 25, to Marija:

I am asking you to pray now because Satan is strong and he wants to take away as many souls as possible.

Pray, dear children, and trust me more because I am here to help you and guide you on a new way towards a new life.

That is why, dear little children, listen and live what I tell you because it is important to you, when I will not be with you anymore, that you will remember my words and all I told you.

Again I invite you to start changing your life, and to decide to convert, not with words, but with your life.

November 13, brief encouragement message transmitted by Marija to the member of Salice Termi's retreat.

November 25:

Today more than ever, I invite you to pray. May your whole life become prayer. Without love, one cannot pray. That is why I invite you to first love God, Creator of your life. Then you will recognize God, and you will love Him completely as He loves you.

Dear children, the fact that I am with you is a grace; that is why, accept and live my messages for your well being. I love you, and that is why I am with you - to teach you and to lead you in a new life of conversion and renouncement. Only then will you discover God and all that is now far away from you.

December 13, Monday, 10:00 p.m., to Ivan, on the hill of Podbrdo:

Tonight, your Mother wants to invite you, very especially, to renew family prayer. During this family prayer, dear children, read more of the Bible, especially the passages that concern the time [of Advent]. Pray, dear children, especially in this time [of tests], and through praying, prepare for the great day that is coming. May this Christmas be different from the other Christmases; may it be more joyous, dear children. Remember how we were happy in the stable when my Son was born. May your family be as happy as those who were present in the stable.

December 25, to Marija:

Today, I want to take you all under my umbrella and protect you from satanic attacks.

Today is the day of peace; but in the whole world, peace is sorely missing. That is why I call upon you to build with me, through prayer, a new world of peace; this I cannot do without you. It is why I call all of you with my love as a Mother, and God will do the rest. Thus open yourself up to God's plan and to His purposes so that you can collaborate with Him for peace and goodness.

Do not forget that your life is not yours, but a gift through which you must radiate joy for others and guide them toward eternal Life.

Dear children, may my sweet Jesus' wisdom be with you always.

January 25:

Today, I invite you to live and accept the messages seriously. Now are some days during which you make a decision for God, peace and goodness. May all hate and jealousy disappear from your life and your thought, and may only the love of God and your brother be there.

Thus, only thus, will you be able to discern the signs of this time. I am with you, and I guide you towards a new era - an era God gives you as a grace to know Him even better.

February 25:

Dear children, today I bless you with my motherly benediction, and I invite you to decide to change your life and work more in the Church, not with words or thoughts, but by example. It is my desire. May your life be a joyous testimony of Jesus. You will not say that you are converted, but your life must become an everyday conversion. To understand what you must do, my children, pray, and God will make you understand what to do concretely, and where you need to change.

I am with you, and I take you under my umbrella.

March 18, to Mirjana, for her 12th annual apparition:

Dear children, give me your hand. It is my desire, and thus I will be able to lead you as a Mother on the true way to the Father. Open your heart and let me in. Pray, because in prayer I am with you. Pray, and let yourself be led. It is peace and happiness to which I lead you.

March 25:

Today, like never before, I ask you to pray for peace: peace in your heart, in your family and in the whole world, because Satan wants war. He wants the absence of peace; he wants to destroy all that is good. That is why, dear children, pray, pray, pray.

April 25:

Today, I invite you to awaken your heart to love. Go see nature and how it awakens. It will help you to open your heart to God, the Creator's love.

My desire is that you awaken the love in your families so that where there is peace, not hate, love can reign. And when love is in your heart, then prayer is also there. Do not forget, dear children, that I am with you and that I help you with my prayer so that God can give you the strength to love.

I bless you and love you with my motherly love.

May 25:

Today, I invite you to open up to God with prayer so that the Holy Spirit starts miracles in you and around you.

I am with you, and I intercede with God for each of you because, dear children, each one of you is important in my plan for Salvation.

I invite you to be bearers of Good and Peace. God wants to give you peace only if you convert and pray. That is why, my dear little children, Pray, Pray, Pray and do all the Holy Spirit will inspire in you.

WAR: LOVE YOUR ENEMIES

8

CONCLUSION AND FUTURE

Medjugorje is being put to the test from all sides. This is often true when God's humble grace converts hearts and disturbs the thinking of the "wise", whether they be theologians or servants of the ecclesiastic administration. The highbrows characterize the messages as crazy, thus illusory. They close their eyes to the fruits of those simple words that become life for the heart. Many of brilliant intelligence do not know anymore what a mother and life are. However, we must read the messages at the level of these simple basics in order to be enlightened. The basic words become reality in action; they inspire creativity and freedom. Such is the originality of these messages. They reveal their meaning and enlightenment in a lived engagement. They bring back to life essential words from the forgotten Gospel.

"Genocide" could describe the destruction resulting from the war. Medjugorje has become a refuge, even for the Blue Helmets who have been staying there a long time. Prayer and action must follow efforts towards the peace that will succeed someday.

To some the messages seem insignificant and are apparently contradicted by this war. Those who live them, however, understand with Our Lady that the war and the atrocities in Bosnia-Hercegovina do not come from God, but from Man. Prayer and fasting have not mobilized our hearts enough to neutralize the grave effects of this destructive tidal wave of sin. The results are practical atheism, God's death in our hearts, and the unrestrained liberation of the craziest desires: food, eroticism, violence, possession, knowledge without wisdom, domination by people who seem magical and take everything from the outside. Murders are multiplying: wars, violence, and abortions, the latter encouraged by laws that condemn conscientious objection to its practice.

The Gospel teaches us that we acknowledge God's gifts from our interiors. All life (animal and plant) and thought develop from the inside in contrast to industry which builds from the outside. Industry does have some worth and efficiency, but sometimes it destroys man when it is systematically applied to his life. Do our good ministers, who, in good conscience, inaugurated the condom vending machine that promotes promiscuity in the high schools, ever consider how such a measure could stimulate a blind libertinism that degrades love and promotes "transmissible sexual" diseases? They seem to ignore that, according to research and surveys, condoms are often inefficient as was verified with the brand "Satan" (genially baptized this name but technically defective). Undisciplined eroticism often frees itself from condoms, as the most serious research reveals. To hide the sad results of their reassuring advice, these proponents of safe sex accuse the Pope of being a propagator of AIDS because he advocates other means which are recognized as efficient by truly scientific research. This is only one example of the inefficient manner in which our technological civilization attempts to resolve human problems.

More specifically, according to the Gospel, order comes from the heart, and life avoids evil from the inside. Jesus has already said, "*Everyone who looks at a woman with lust has already committed adultery with her in his heart*" (Mt 5, 28). He has invited us to radically orient and master our desires by uniting with God and the constant inspiration of the Holy Spirit.

Christ and Our Lady's small flock has understood and committed itself to prayer and fasting which inspire us to help others. The future is on its way. The spiritual fight, which had its paroxysm during the Passion of Christ, continues. It is from the inside that Our Lady leads us to victory.

Vicka, upon her return from a large meeting in Holland, said:

We live a time of grace, but many people do not understand. They have put the fear of war in first place. They are worried about material considerations. They are blind and do not see the proof that there are neither any casualties nor destruction here in Medjugorje. The messages must be in first place; only then will we be able to discover how this time is a time of grace.

WAR: LOVE YOUR ENEMIES

9

TWELFTH ANNIVERSARY: JUNE 24-25, 1993

The international crowd

On June 24-25, 1993, Medjugorje celebrated, in spite of the Moslems' threats of war, the 12th anniversary of the apparitions in peace and deep joy.

Many pilgrims had gone against their friends and family's advice: *"Don't go, it's too dangerous."*

The pilgrims ignored them in order to bring their support to this country at war and to Our Lady's project. They did not have to suffer for it.

The pilgrimage on which I went had only one incident. The plane from Air Provence, chartered by Genevieve Bastard, was packed with 133 pilgrims and 4 tons of humanitarian relief. When the plane approached the town, the landing was not authorized. Instead we were sent to Rome where we spent 24 hours in prolonged suspense. While the 133 pilgrims were praying, we were calling everywhere. The negotiations were difficult to do from airport phones where nobody could call us. We were finally able to reach the United Nations, the Ministries, the French Embassy and the General Consulate in Rome who were very cooperative. After a long wait, everything was arranged. Our powerful protectors told us that the problem with the authorities in Zagreb was coming from private interests opposed to the private pilgrimage organized by Genevieve Bastard herself (a pilgrimage which was outside of their very well established jurisdiction) and to the tons of food relief she brings regularly.

Once again like in the great days of 20 to 30,000 pilgrims, Medjugorje found a crowd consisting of 4,000 Americans, more than 1,000 Italians, more than 500 French, 150 Australians, 50 from the Far East and so on.

It was very serene in the shadow of Our Lady. We seemed very far from the spirits which everyday offer massive objection: *"It has lasted 12 years; thus it must be false!"*

Those who say such things judge by exteriors. They contrast Medjugorje to the brief apparitions, which are without any doubt exemplary, like Lourdes or especially Pontmain and La Salette where there was only one apparition. The objectors forget that all along the Church's life, many visionaries have benefited from exceptional phenomenon right up to their death, in accordance with their mission. Benoite Rencurel, visionary of Our Lady of Laus, had communications with the Holy Virgin from May 1664 up to her death on December 28, 1718, more than 54 years.

The 12 years of Medjugorje have accumulated many spiritual laurels: more confessions, more conversions, and more healings medically supervised at different levels. But especially today, in the horror of the war, the visionaries live love for the enemy without failing.

The quality of the pilgrims has again impressed me. These people, often Medjugorje converts, pray intensely and deeply. As a priest, I am sensitive to their incredible receptivity, and also to the quality of the liturgical participation assisted by the musical interpretations of the Community of the Beatitudes. The people, even the more elderly ones, accept gracefully the tiring and uncomfortable conditions. The heat is intolerable. There is no planned lunch. Sleep is often interrupted. The rooms for 2 often bring on problems (snoring, etc.). They accept all this without complaint or argument while paying attention to each other. Their abandonment to God and Our Lady inspires everyone.

The peace march (June 14)

A second peace march occurred on Thursday, June 24. Last year, the 12 km procession, from Humac (the Franciscan novitiate) to the Church of Medjugorje, started under a German's initiative, Hubert Liebherr. This year, 2 to 3,000 people got together at 11 o'clock in the morning; and Monsignor Franic, 80 year old emeritus Archbishop of Split, gave the starting signal and guided the first five kilometers. Vicka, with a red cap under the sparkling sun, led the group with her powerful singing and unalterable smile, in spite of diverse signs showing some health problems.

Before the start, the crowd heard the tragic testimony from Travnik's refugees. In that town, which is attributed to the Croatians under the Owen plan, the Moslems proceeded with one of their ethnic cleansings about which the French press keep silent. Only the Serbs' and Croatians' ethnic cleansings have been publicized. At the moment of expulsion, a woman had received her son's body, a soldier. She was without news of her other son, also mobilized, and her two daughters. The crowd cried while listening to her. This testimony and others showed the new situation in Bosnia-Hercegovina. For a long time, the Moslems, not well armed, had been primarily victims of international diplomacy and the Serbs. The Owen plan gave them bare minimum existence. Now, with more weapons, they are attacking, having been stimulated by the influx of volunteers coming from Africa and Asia and helped by the Moudjahins from Moslem countries. Their leaders have understood that the United Nations approved their actions. They are now engaged in their own ethnic cleansing. This new tactic has given them more weight with the international authorities and the press. If the Owen plan favored the Serbs and in turn the Croatians, the new plans, which have been published since June 1993, are radically against the Croatians. They would not have territories in the North anymore. They would only keep a small part in the South, in Hercegovina, with Mostar its capital strangely placed on the border. The Moslems, whom the Croatians supported against the Serbs, have now turned against their allies of yesterday. Conflicts rage in Mostar and elsewhere at the time I write.

The Medjugorje men, all mobilized since the beginning of the war, had not one casualty until now, in contrast to other villages. In this overwhelming hell, this protection seems over; a 20 year old young man was killed on July 5.

In the whole of Bosnia-Hercegovina, where the horror grows, the Serbs have imposed tax on humanitarian relief, and their troops often attack the convoys. The one point that seems in common among the several divisions of the United Nations is that the Serbs keep the lion's share.

The mass of June 24, 1993

On the eve of June 24, more than 130 priests celebrated mass with Archbishop Franic. Father Jozo Zovko preached on Medjugorje's miracles, the most incredible one being this mass blessed by deep conversions and generosity.

-*Stay alive; do not imitate cadavers*, he basically concluded.

He was directing his comments to the diplomacy which has only been successful at prolonging the conflict and endorsing injustice.

On the afternoon of June 25 ("which is, for the Holy Virgin, the anniversary date of her first apparition on the hill"), Ivanka, who received the 10th secret in 1985 and who now receives only one apparition per year, came before her 8th annual apparition in the intimacy of the familial house. Her two children accompanied her. I was admitted, thanks to Mr. Pellegrino Pedrochi, Ivanka's usual host during her pilgrimages.

The apparition was shorter, 7 minutes, and in a different style from those of the preceding years. At the end of the three Rosaries, Ivanka, in her flowered celebration dress, entered with her whole family. The crowd of some 60 people packed in the living room made room for them and tried to place themselves as close as possible to Ivanka, facing the wall, which interfered with the videos. Only the Italian Television found a good spot. After the recitation of several Aves and Paters, Ivanka, who had been standing up high from her size, kneeled quickly in the transparent joy of reunion. But soon she started to cry. In tears she said aloud the Our Father and Gloria with the Gospa and the whole crowd.

After 7 minutes, she lowered her head and the apparition was over. She prayed one more moment then departed rapidly, without summarizing the message like she first did in preceding years. Friends stopped her to ask her, and she only said:

-The Holy Virgin showed me horrible things which will come soon. She asks us to give ourselves to Her Son through prayer.

Some dramatized the event. But, on the following day, Ivanka specified to Sister Emmanuel:

-What I saw does not concern the secrets. It is like a new warning because these grave things can still be changed by praying and fasting, conversion and abandonment to Jesus. These are more important than ever. Do not remain blind; convert.

Marija's message

Some had announced that the 12th anniversary message would be extraordinary, but it turned out to only be an insistent rerun of the usual message. Prayer remains the true urgency in a material world left to elementary desires; and, in spite of quantities of good intentions, the actions of numerous elite do not compensate for the failure of the masses who seem complacent and anesthetized by television shows everyday. These are the reasons behind this anniversary message:

> *Today again, I rejoice from your presence here; I give you my benediction as a Mother, and I intercede for each one of you with God. I ask you again to live the messages and to realize them in your life. I am with you, and I give you my benediction everyday.*
>
> *Dear children, these times are exceptional; and it is why I am with you, to love you and protect you, to take Satan away from your heart and to bring you closer to my Son Jesus' Heart.*

10

TEXTS AND FILES

1. MARIJA
November 1986 interview published in June 1992

This interview, unpublished for a long time, was finally printed in Caritas, Birmingham, USA.

Heaven

Question - Did you go to Heaven, or did you see Heaven?
Marija - I have seen Heaven; but Jakov, Ivan and Vicka took me there.
Q - Where were you when you had this apparition?
M - In Jakov's house.
Q - You saw Heaven? Did it look like a place or a state?
M - It was like when you see a film on a screen or when you look out the window. I had an apparition. I was not there like the other visionaries.
Q - Did you feel like you were strolling through the woods, or was the apparition spiritual or picturesque?
M - Before, I had never seen such a scene. No one can even begin to imagine what it is like.
Q - Were there people surrounding the flowers you saw?
[Marija has already talked about flowers before the interview]
M - Yes, they were around the flowers. They were all the same age; no one in Heaven is older than Christ (33 years old). In Heaven, people are full of joy, and all thank God for his gifts. Everyday, they realize a little more how much God loves them.
Q - Were there many?
M - Yes, many.

Q - Were there any buildings?

M - *No.*

Q - Were there any streets?

M - *No, only flowers.*

Q - Was Jesus with these people?

M - *We did not see Him.*

Jesus' apparition

Q - You did not see Him even in other apparitions?

M - *I did; we saw Jesus once, hurting from His Passion.*

Q - Can you describe Him?

M - *We saw His bust [from His waist]. It was an unclear image, and His face was showing pain. It was the first year of the apparitions, when we all [the visionaries] had lots of problems. Our Lady showed her Son to encourage us to be brave and to suffer , like Jesus suffered, and to give.*

Q - At Christmas, did you see Our Lady with the Infant Jesus?

M - *Yes, every Christmas, Mary comes with the Infant Jesus in her arms.*

Q - Did she let you touch Him?

M - *No.*

Q - Did you want to?

Q - *Yes.*

To touch

Q - Did you ask Our Lady for permission to touch Him?

M - *We only asked Our Lady to touch her, and she allowed us only once.*

Q - What did you feel when you touched her?

M - *It's impossible to describe. Words are meaningless to describe the experience. Each touch produced great joy. It was an impression and a feeling impossible to describe with words.*

Q - Touching Her was thus incredible?

M- *Yes, we felt a very special joy, our Mother's particular love when we were touching her.*

Q - During the later apparitions, Our Lady told you to go to the Blue Cross, when the authorities were watching over the hill. Did you often go to that refuge? When you were there, were there only visionaries or other people as well?

M - *Yes, we often had apparitions at the Blue Cross because the authorities had forbidden us to go to the hill. Since we were going up, Our Lady told us, "Do not go; the police are there. Stay here [on the Blue Cross site]. And it is there that I will come".*

Q - Did Our Lady appear here in your house?

M - *Sometimes, when one of the visionaries is ill, she will appear in his home.*

Q - Did you have this experience? Was it in your bedroom?

M - *Yes.*

The sign

Q - Be specific; will the great sign that is to be given to all non-believers occur on the hill of the apparitions behind us (Marija's house), or in another place?

M - *Our Lady told us that she will leave a sign on the hill of the apparitions.*

Q - What can you tell us about the sign Our Lady promised to leave us?

M - *It will be a visible sign, for all non-believers, because those who already believe do not need this sign.*

Q - The matter is not clear. Will the sign come after the end of the apparitions or after the punishment?

M - *I could not say.*

Purgatory

Q - When you had your apparition of Heaven, did you also have an apparition of Purgatory?

M - *I had all these apparitions [Heaven, Purgatory, Hell] at the same time.*

Q - It has been said there were 12 levels in Purgatory. Is that true?

M - *We saw Purgatory as a whole, from the same place, not from levels. And it was misty. We heard many voices who asked for our prayers, because when they were on earth, they did not recognize God's existence. They were unsure of God. But now they know God exists, and they await our prayers to help them enter Heaven some day.*

Q - What do they do in Purgatory?

M - *It was so misty that we could not see, but we are certain they suffer much. In Purgatory, they know of God and have great need of our prayers. Our Lady tells the visionaries to tell people to often pray for them, so that they can be transferred to Heaven.*

Q - Then, you did not see clearly, but could hear better?

M - *Yes.*

Hell

Q -Did Our Lady reveal to you if a soul from Purgatory was lost and would go Hell?

M - *No, once they are in Purgatory they can only go to Heaven.*

Q - In your opinion, will the people who go from worse to worse, or from evil to good, and who still love God, go to Hell?

M - *I do not know. When a man dies, God gives him special graces and benedictions to let him decide where he wants to go. God shows him an image of his life and what he has done during that life, and thus He gives him the grace to decide where he will go, according to what his life was. He has free choice.*

This supports the experience of some dying people who see their life before their eyes, instantly, with a clear judgment of good and evil.

Q - Well, you want to avoid Hell and go to Heaven. What happens in that case [...]?

M - *God gives us special graces to completely understand and thus answer with the truth.*

Q - Thus, He gives us many graces to say, "God, I want to go to Heaven and I want to avoid Hell or Purgatory" (like a truth scrum)?

M - *Yes, that's it.*

Q - When you saw Hell, you saw a young girl who was keeping close to the flames. Did you see her face? [Marija had talked about this girl before the taped interview].

M - *We saw her in Hell, and she was in the flames. She came out and there was something animalistic about her face. Something wild.*

Q - In Hell, when you saw this girl, did Our Lady tell you why she was there?

M - *She did not tell us.*

Q- Is she the only person you saw?

M - *No, there were many people. But we noticed her because she was caught in the flames.*

Q - Was she in a lot of pain?

M - *All those in Hell were running to avoid the flames. There was much pain. But God gives each one the freedom of where to go. Those people had chosen Hell.*

Q - Then God does not send anyone to Hell; they decide it for themselves?

M - *Yes, we are judge of our life.*

Q - When you saw hell, did you see Satan himself and other demons?

M - *I had one apparition of Hell. I was not present.*

Q - Yes, but in your apparition, did you see demons or Lucifer?

M - We were not able to see Satan; but Mirjana, another visionary, who lives in Sarajevo, saw Him once [...], as a beautiful young man. Mirjana was in her house, and the door was locked. Suddenly a young man appeared. He tried to convince her to renounce the apparitions by promising her all the world's riches if she did. But she took some Holy Water to sign herself and he disappeared. Then Our Lady appeared immediately and talked to her.

Q - She had then realized it was the demon?

M - Yes.

Q - Were Satan's promises vain, or did he really have the power to make them come true? Did she think he had that power? Because anybody can make such promises.

M - Yes, yes, the demon has such great powers. And it was a great temptation for Mirjana. She felt her strength leave her.

Q - Thus she went through a great temptation?

M - Yes, a big one.

The future

Q - What about you, Marija, did you ask Our Lady if you would go to Heaven like Jacinta, Francisco and Lucie did in Fatima? They asked Our-Lady, "Will we go to Heaven?" And She told them, "Yes."

M - No, we did not ask her.

Q - Were you afraid to?

M - I would prefer Paradise, through its door...

The Pope

Q - In the USA, there are many protests, and many do not accept what the Holy Father says. Do you have something to say on the matter? Even some Catholics of good faith think the Pope goes against their conscience.

M - *The Good Mother asked the visionaries and all the people to pray for the Holy Father and listen to him.*

Q - Did you have direct or indirect contact with the Pope?

M - *Once, Our Lady gave me a message for the Pope. It was given to him [by the Archbishop of Parma].*

Q - Did you get an answer?

M - *Yes, he gave me his benediction.*

Q - Do you know if, personally, he believes in the Medjugorje apparitions?

M - *Yes, we are sure he believes in them. He told a group of Italian bishops during a pilgrimage in Rome that he would like to go to Medjugorje, but it was not officially convenient.*

Q - Do you know how long these apparitions will last?

M - *Our Lady did not tell us.*

2. A HOMOSEXUAL'S SPIRITUAL HEALING

I want to testify on the healing I received from Our Lady in Medjugorje.

I am a 65 year old single man. When I was 17 years of age, I entered the Franciscan Order as a novice brother. After about 2 years the time came for the temporary vows. But since I had a hard time being chaste, in spite of considerable effort, I decided it was better to leave. At 20 years of age, I was introduced to the gay life, and soon after I committed myself to this life style. It lasted 40 years. During this time, I went to mass every Sunday, but without confession nor the Eucharist not even at Easter.

At age 60, I was still working on conduits (my profession) in a Catholic church, and in the entrance, I saw a copy of Wayne Weible's Journal on Medjugorje. I had vaguely heard about children who were seeing Our Lady in Yugoslavia, but it was my first information on Medjugorje. Most likely a parishioner had left the copy there. It was in December of 1987; information on Medjugorje was rare here in Los Angeles.

I took the journal home; and that night, after dinner, I read the whole thing with great interest. Our Lady says that the time to convert is short; that great graces would be given rapidly for conversion. She would heal all sorts of constraints. You just had to follow her message. Such was the meaning of the article.

I was greatly impressed by this story. Rather surprisingly, I did not have a hard time believing it.

That night, before going to bed, I kneeled and asked Our Lady:

-Well, if you want to heal me of all of my sexual problems and keep me completely chaste, as you say you can, I promise that I will completely follow the message you gave in Medjugorje. If you do that for me, I want to do that for you. OK?

I went to bed with a small reticence in my mind. I did not think it would work.

During the following days, I started fasting on bread and water, which I had never done in my life. And I started praying often, especially the Rosary. The temptations became worse than before. The first six months and even the first year were hell, or so it seemed to me. I doubted I could hold. I could hardy pray, but I was like Saint-Peter, when he felt himself sinking in the water and was saying: "Lord, save me". Think how stupid I felt, when I saw myself staying chaste in spite of temptations and Satan. Yes I was stupid to have first doubted what Our Lady wanted and could do.

How did She do it? Well! How to explain this miracle? Impossible! By seeing how it happened to me, I can only say that it is through Our Lady's powerful intercession that I received this gift from the Holy Spirit. He gave me the power to overcome Satan's terrible traps. I was motivated. From where did it come? The Holy Spirit is like a breath. We do not know from where it comes, but we certainly know when He does it.

And it has been lasting for the last 5 years. I have remained completely chaste since that night when I kneeled in front of my bed to ask my Mother this favor. I take the sacrament each day, and I feel a calling for the apostolate to help those who suffer from similar problems.

Since my conversion in 1987, I have visited Medjugorje three times during pilgrimages. Pray, pray, pray.

– Donald L. Kohles, Los Angeles, CA

PS. If Father Laurentin wants to use my testimony, he can summarize or paraphrase it according to his judgment [I did a literal translation]. He can use my name or initials. He has my authorization. (May 5, 1992).

3. HOW MILONA OF HAPSBURG BECAME A MULTILINGUAL SECRETARY IN MEDJUGORJE

Discreet, simple and modest she may be, but many notice that the presbyter in Medjugorje has benefited from a high class secretary, able to easily answer in most known languages. Many did not know that she was a princess, descending from the Hungarian branch of the House of Hapsburg - the royal House of Austria. Marc Waterinck has received the story of her conversion, published in Echo 97.

It was at the occasion of a party with friends that I first heard about Medjugorje. I felt right away that I had to go there. In 3 days, my whole life changed. While I was climbing Krizevac, between the 5th and 6th stations of the Way of the Cross, I sat apart from the group, exhausted. I was there, sitting on a stone. I was thinking, and I felt a presence. My eyes remained fixed upon the Church of Medjugorje clearly visible below in the plain. That is when I clearly saw the church roof open and the sky being engulfed inside. It lasted long enough for me to understand it physically: Medjugorje will diffuse the sky to the whole universe. I saw all the problems and important questions in my life; and at the same time I was thinking:

-If Medjugorje is real, then you, what are you doing with your life? If God truly exists, how do you pretend to be a Christian?

A priest passed by, and with him I started climbing again. When I arrived, I confessed. A sincere penitence had seized my heart and made me cry. Three days later, I left Medjugorje; but a great fire burned in me. After that experience, everything I did would take on a different meaning. I had an incredible desire to go back to Medjugorje. I went back and stayed a few months. A year later, I got rid of everything I had. My friend thought I was crazy. But I left everything behind.

I learned that Father Slavko needed a secretary and an interpreter. I went there for three months. Now I have been here for seven years. God has taken up my whole life, and my conversion is in continuing development. I have the impression that before that experience, I did not have faith, although raised as a Christian. Before, I believed God was some place on the clouds, while today I live with Him. I do not see God, but He is closer and more real than the people who live around me.

I have discovered God's love beyond human logic, in the fight against my ego and against sin. I feel it important to pray for those who stay with Satan, that is all, and to also pray for the visionaries and the priests of Medjugorje, so that the grace received here spreads among men.

4. A PROTESTANT MINISTER,
MEDJUGORJE'S APOSTLE

Wayne Weible is the most active promoter of Medjugorje throughout the United States, with conferences, books, tapes and journals. He has talked about his conversion, which is also a discovery of Catholic plenitude. Here is his essential story.

In October 1985, I was at a cross roads. A young Lutheran journalist from Myrtle Beach (South Carolina), owner of four periodicals, I was just divorced and was starting a new life with a new family. I was so irritated with God that I was not going to Church anymore. That is when the Holy Virgin grabbed me.

That evening of October 1985, I was waiting for Terry, my spouse, to finish putting the children to bed. I had planned to watch a video on the apparitions of Medjugorje with her. I was skeptical. But it was being discussed a lot, and it could make an article. When the visionaries' ecstasy started on the screen, all of my journalistic objectivity jumped.

I moved my head back and forth saying, "Incredible!"

And I felt in my heart that I was believing it. I even had the sensation that somebody was talking to me. It was more like an inner voice, not perceptible by ear. I do not know how I was so certain it was the Holy Virgin.

That voice was saying: "You are my son, and I ask you to do my Son's will."

I was looking at Terry. Had she also heard? She was watching the screen with interest, but relaxed. But I thought I was dying. The message continued:

-Write the facts on Medjugorje. If you accept, it will become your life mission. You will cease your present activity.

The rest of the video was lost in a fog. But how do I tell my wife, "The Holy Virgin asked me to spread this message?" I was speechless. She was looking at me smiling: "Hey, why don't you take an aspirin and go to bed? Tomorrow morning, you will be fresh."

Nothing in my previous experiences had prepared me for such an event. There were only two possibilities: I was going crazy, or I really had received a message. And the alternative presented even greater difficulties. Jesus Christ had suddenly become a reality - a true Jesus, in flesh and bone, alive today. And His Mother, who appeared to children, had talked to me.

I fell on my knees and I started praying like I had never prayed before in my life. I was overwhelmed by what had happened and did not know how to obey Mary's requests. Finally, I plucked up courage, and I sat down with the resolution to write my first article; but I remained sitting there as if paralyzed by my inability to fill up the page.

At that time, I felt the message in my heart again:

-Pray more, study more.

I obeyed the message and started praying aloud.

-Lord, I do not understand what is happening to me, nor why; but I will look for an answer.

I had decided to do what had been asked of me. Even if it meant weeks of research, I was ready. It took me some time to find some files (there are no Catholic libraries in North Carolina). Finally, I found a history of the Marian apparitions from the 16th century up to our time. I was surprised to learn that there had been apparitions for 19 centuries. Thus Medjugorje was not a new thing. It belonged to a tradition. But never had the Madonna appeared with such frequency, during such a long period and to so many visionaries at the same time. Finally, I felt ready to write. As I was inserting the paper in the typewriter, I felt the need for praying:

-Thanks, Lord, whatever I must do, please, help me. Ideas came one after another, my fingers were flying on the keyboard.

After that, I abandoned my activities. I dedicated myself completely to the spreading of the message of Medjugorje. My first 8 articles were put together and 32 million copies were made in different languages. Only Christ and Mary counted. I decided to sell the four journals I owned and abandon my profession, knowing the risks. And then one evening, I called George Matt, Director General of a business which owned 29 weekly journals. He asked me if I were interested in selling my 4 journals. It came as a shock since I had tried to sell them for 2 years. But I had never had any interesting offer. Then the Holy Virgin's words came back to me: "You will not continue your usual activity."

I told Terry, "I just sold the journals. The message is coming true." She looked at me as if she did not know if she was supposed to cry, laugh or scream.

My faith was confirmed by signs received during my first trip to Medjugorje. I was going through a radical conversion; however, I was ignoring the Rosary. Then a lady from the Catholic parish called. She asked me for copies of my articles and added:

-My sisters and I have a small gift for you, if you would like to come get it.

I promised to go. I met Mrs. Afford:

-Here: would you accept this Rosary. It comes from Fatima.
-Thanks, but what must I do?
She smiled.
-It is true, you are Protestant and you do not know the Rosary. This little book will teach you what to do.

Before these events, I only prayed 5 minutes a week. I was looking for the way to prayer. I discovered the beauty and the power of this prayer; I had never felt a deeper sensation than speaking with God. I was going from discovery to discovery.

One day, I entered a church, and my eyes fell on the confessionals. During the whole day, I had thought about confessing. To me, a Lutheran, it was a totally new thing. We Lutherans do it publicly, but I was stricken by the large number of pilgrims waiting in line to confess. They were worried about cleansing their soul, some for the first time in years. I wanted it too, but I was Protestant. What to do? I stopped resisting; I got up and went towards the church exit. As I was passing the Italian confessional, a large and strong priest who was standing very near whispered:

-Italian?
-No, English, I answered, while moving away.

But with a radiant smile upon his face, he took my shoulders and pushed me into the confessional, where a small paper said, "English."
-Well, my son? *The priest started gently.*
He was waiting and I was waiting. I did not know what to say. Finally I mumbled:

-I would like to confess, but I do not know how. I have never done it. I am Protestant.

You are what?

The priest got closer.

-I am Protestant, Father, I repeated.

My knees were hurting. My only desire was to get up and leave. He looked at me intensely and said:

-I will hear your confession, but I can only absolve Catholics.

-Father, I do not know what to do.

He shook his head and said:

-I will say the Commandments and you will simply answer yes or no.

I felt elevated when he got to "thou shall not kill". I finally was able to answer, "No."

My legs were shaking. I was deeply moved, I felt extraordinarily purified; I had never felt such a thing. I started to think about what had happened and to laugh. That poor priest! I did not know which one of us had been the most shaken.

The Holy Virgin also made me discover Jesus in the Eucharist, and now I can not tolerate to be deprived of it.

On the fourth trip (July 1987), the Holy Virgin clearly told me:

-Go outside, among the crowd and do what you promised to do.

And I understood that being God's messenger is a 24 hour a day, 365 day a year engagement.

Wayne's mission has been fruitful. Nobody ignores Medjugorje any more in the United States. He contributed to the extraordinary development of 180 Medjugorje Centers, with many prayer groups affiliated to each one of them. He is invited to the great conferences on Medjugorje, like the one for Our Lady with 7,000 participants. His book has been translated into numerous languages. Dino Lunetti, Marija's future father-in-law, was his editor in Italian.

The last time I saw him, he felt a little torn between his role as a Protestant journalist and Medjugorje propagandist who is welcomed with much tolerance and openness. His growing attraction for the Eucharist, the holy Virgin and the Rosary integrated him to Catholicism. His experience is similar to Max Thurian's, who had been one of the first leaders of the COE in Geneva and who became a Catholic priest in Naples. Even in the discreet way he did it, he could not avoid a stir. The Protestants, remarkably tolerant, reacted tactfully. It was Max Thurian's Catholic friends who were the most severe and reproached him as an "Ecumenical indelicacy". I talked about just such a problem with Wayne Weible about a year or two ago, after a conference where I had admired not only his sincerity and his ardor, but also his talent as a speaker and leader.

5. INTERVIEWS OF 3 VISIONARIES

BY THE INFORMATEUR DE MONTREAL: OCTOBER 7, 1992

These 3 interviews occurred in the rotunda built behind the Church of Medjugorje. Since visionaries often repeat the same essential things to pilgrims, we only kept a few facts which we felt presently deserve attention.

Before the interview, each visionary said. with the interviewers, a *Pater*, an *Ave* and a *Gloria*, followed by the *Queen of Peace* invocation.

Marija

By Her presence here, the Holy Virgin wants to help us change evil into good. That is why She asks us to live the messages She gave us. She introduced herself as the Queen of Peace and invited us to ask for the peace that comes from God. Before all, peace must come down into our heart through contact with God. Once established in ourselves, this peace can spread to our family. And then, [...] we can pray for peace in the world.

Here, we experience war. It has taught us a little more about the meaning of the message. The Holy Virgin prepared us for this situation. Unfortunately, we did not act enough on Her demands. This war is our people's cross to bear. See the youth's suffering, who die or have arms and legs amputated. On the other hand, many people are spiritually reborn and get closer to God. Through suffering, we are showered with many graces.

The Holy Virgin has taught us to live in prayer, because without prayer we cannot do anything. [...] The Rosary is the prayer she prefers. She also recommended the Bible, to give it a very visible place in our home. She invites us to unify ourselves, through prayer, so that our meeting at work or elsewhere is prayer. She asks everybody to choose that way. Skin color or other distinctions are not important. Because all of us are called. [...]

Changing our lives is not enough. Our habits must also changed. When we are in the church, She says, we are like saints; but when we leave the church, we act like pagans. She asks us to act as of people who live with God.

The Holy Virgin insists that with prayer and fasting we can beat the war. She asks for fasting on bread and water on Wednesday and Friday [...]. She would like us to offer our fasting to God with love, and to abandon sins.

She asks us to confess a least once a month. [...] She suggests that we meet Jesus at mass. The most beautiful thing is to meet God at the Holy Mass.

Vicka

Vicka - At the beginning, when Our Lady talked, we did not know She was alluding to a war that concerned us. We thought she was talking about a far away place. But by the expression on Her face, we finally understood she was talking about our country. Not at the beginning. Only later.

Question - You did not have a normal childhood. Do you regret it?

V - No, I do not regret one moment. It was never hard. I am very happy that Our Lady chose me as an instrument to help others. I regret nothing.

Q - Is the illness you suffer from right now and for which you receive treatments mystical like it was the case in 1988?

V - I do not believe it to be mystical. God simply uses people to suffer in the place of others. If He uses me, He can use anybody else. He wants to teach us the acceptance of suffering.

Q - The Apocalypse says that the Devil will be in chain one day. Is that only symbolic?

V - I believe Satan will be defeated only if we accept the Gospa's messages. If we convert and live like the Gospa teaches us, then we will have a period of peace. It depends on us. If we do not change, it will not happen.

Q - Then this reign of peace is not purely symbolic?

V - Obviously it is for this earth.

Q - Has the Holy Virgin's attitude changed since the beginning of the war?

V - Of course, there has been a change in attitude. You can see it in the expression on her face. At the beginning of the apparitions, She always had a joyous face, smiling. Later on, sadness could be seen on her face. Ivan and Marija saw Her cry. Myself, I have seen her very sad.

Q - And now, how is She?

V - *Not too happy, nor too sad - in between.*

Q - Do you believe that the last events mentioned in the Apocalypse have started to happen?

V - *I cannot say anything about that, because Our Lady has said nothing specific. Thus I do not know.*

Q - Many people believe that it is the beginning of the end.

V - *It could be, but the Holy Virgin has said nothing on that subject.*

Mirjana

Mirjana - *The first time we saw Our Lady, we could not understand what was happening. We thought we were going crazy. And when I told my mother that I had saw Our Lady, her first question was 'Are you normal?' [she laughs]*

At the beginning we were very excited, but at the same time it was difficult to accept. [...] However, when later on we understood that it was our Mother, it became a lot easier. As a bishop underlined lately, what we understood then was not the fact that Mary is the Mother of us all (She is, of course), but that She is my Mother, My own Mom. This prevails in our relationship with the Holy Virgin. She always stands next to us and answers our prayers.

Eliane [a person present at the interview] - Medjugorje's adversaries saw a bad sign in the fact that you were first afraid. Don't celestial apparitions always bring peace?

M - *[sharply]. - Of course we felt peace. But at the same time, we were very nervous because we did not understand what was happening at all. It was beyond comprehension. We were not prepared. (We did not know about Lourdes and Fatima). We felt a whole mix of feelings.*

Q - Was it difficult when you first started fasting?

M - Before Our Lady's apparitions, we were already fasting here on bread and water on Friday. Then when the Holy Virgin asked us to fast on Wednesday and Friday, we only had to add Wednesday. It was not too difficult.

Q - Did you touch the Holy Virgin, like Ivan, and what did you feel?

M - I never touch the Holy Virgin.

Q - Does each visionary have a prayer group, or do they belong to the same group?

M - Each one has a group of 10 to 15 people, sometimes 20 - it depends. My group gets together once a week, on Saturday, and also on the second day of each month.

Q - Does God choose for each one of you a determined vocation, or does He leave you free?

M - In the beginning, God asks us to pray a lot to find our vocation, but He leaves us free to choose. It does not matter what the vocation will be. What is important is that, in our choice, we become Christian models. If, for example, we decide to found a family, this family must be a model for others. It is the same thing if we choose a religious vocation.

Q - Did not the Holy Virgin say at the beginning, "I would like you to be priests and nuns?"

M - On the second or third day of the apparitions, we asked the Holy Virgin what she expected of us. And She answered that we would know in our hearts what we should do later. But She specified that our choice for life does not matter, but we must always be an example for others.

Q -Is there something special planned in your program for the celebration of Our Lady of the Rosary? [October 7, 1992].

M with a smile - Yes, do my duty, which means clean my house and my garden, because I am expecting my cousins today. Of course, we say the Rosary every day.

6. THREE VISIONARIES' ANSWER
TO THE PILGRIMAGE

ORGANIZED BY M. FRICOTEAUX
SUNDAY MARCH 14, 1993

This 80 people pilgrimage, which was to arrive in Split on Thursday 15, was almost canceled. 50 people had canceled at the last minute because of two pieces of information: a French lady had been killed in Sarajevo, and the Serbs threatened to shoot down the planes which dropped relief into Bosnia. Only 30 people were left. Master Fricoteaux improvised a heroic pilgrimage through Venice, 16 hours by bus each way, to get to Medjugorje. The pilgrims, many of which were octogenarians, slept little, ate little, but kept a quality of prayer, exchange, help and exemplary comprehension that left a great mark on me. Together, we met three visionaries - Mirjana, Ivan, and Jakov whose houses are on the border of Biakovici, across the hill.

Mirjana received us in her garden by starting a prayer. Since many questions only confirmed already known answers which were sometimes repeated in the latest news series, I will keep to a few extracts.

Mirjana

R. Laurentin's question - The last time I met you, you told me about the famous writings the Holy Virgin gave you and on which the 120 secrets are written, visible to you only (a particularity that leaves me perplexed). This document was then in your parents' home in Sarajevo. Is it still there?

Mirjana - It is now here, in my home. Soon after receiving it, I showed it to 2 people. They looked at it but without seeing the same thing, without being able to read the secrets like I could.

R.L. - What does happen on the 2nd of each month, in communication with the Holy Virgin?

M - *We pray for a long time, especially for the non-believers. I would rather say, those who have not received the Lord's love. And from this comes most of the world's problems. To pray for the non-believers is also to pray for our future. The Gospa wishes us to put the Rosary back in its place in the family. On the 2nd of the month, I do not receive a message. We pray together.*

R.L. - What happened on the last meeting?

M - *For an hour, we prayed for those who do not know God, from 9:50 a.m. to 10:50 a.m.*

To other questions she answered:

M - *It is prayer from the heart that counts. When you say Our Father, you must really realize that you speak to a father. The important thing is not to ask, but to give. I am going through a hard time, but later, I feel strong.*

R.L. - Does the holy Virgin appear sad or happy?

M - *Her facial expression changes according to what she talks about.*

R.L. - What do you advise in terms of the bread and water fasting on Wednesday and Friday? Is it better to take a small amount of bread? A large amount?

M - *You must not measure, but not take too much.*

R.L. - Do you know the date of the revelation of the secrets?

M - *Yes.*

R.L. - As soon as 1984, you were in a hurry to contact Father Petar, a Franciscan, whose mission is to reveal the secrets when the Holy Virgin authorizes him. Since you already know the late date of these revelations, why do it so early?

M - *As I understood, Father Petar had to prepare himself.*

Ivan especially told us:

> *The main messages are peace, conversion, prayer,*
> *fasting, deep faith and love. It is hard for me to make*
> *others understand with what fantastic quality of love the*
> *Holy Virgin gives messages day by day. She has come,*
> *from the beginning, as Queen of Peace. She added, "My*
> *Son sends me to help you. Dear children, you must make*
> *peace with God, but also between men. My Son sends me*
> *to show you the remedy." She wants to realize this peace*
> *with us. The Holy Virgin did not only appeared for us*
> *Croatians, but for the people of all races. The greatest*
> *sign of these apparitions is the beginning of a spiritual*
> *change in the world. As many people are becoming aware*
> *of their littleness and their feebleness, they try to become*
> *better and to make peace. Being in the Holy Virgin's school*
> *for 11 and a half years, I still tell myself everyday: "You*
> *still have to convert."*
>
> *The conversion is permanent. It not easy to build a*
> *life according to all the values in a difficult world. It de-*
> *pends on us. God puts it in our hands. To me, the princi-*
> *pal messages are prayer and peace.*
>
> *It is often said that the Gospa's messages are repeti-*
> *tive. To me, even when She says, "Pray, pray, pray," I feel*
> *it every time as unique and new. At each apparition, I*
> *realize more and more how incredibly beautiful She is.*
>
> *Only prayer and fasting can stop the war, because*
> *God is all powerful. He wants to do everything, but not*
> *without us. Let's talk less and act more. We put personal*
> *prayer too much aside by resting upon the prayer of the*
> *Church, and that slows down our spiritual way.*

R.L. - Now that there are fewer pilgrims, do you have
more time to work on your garden?

Ivan - Yes, yesterday I plowed.

R.L. - How does the Holy Virgin appear to you?

I - I see her in three dimensions. I speak to her like to you; I can touch her.

R.L. - Did She kiss you?

I - That is private [with a smile].

R.L. - How must you say the Rosary?

I - You must take time, enrich it with prayer, and meditate on the passages from the Bible. If you say it right, you come out full of force and joy - rested.

R.L. - What about fasting?

I - I was the first one to receive the message to fast on Wednesday and Friday on bread and water. It was hard for me at the beginning. It was an eternal fight. Now, I am used to it. It purifies me spiritually and strengthens my faith. But fasting is not only about food; you can fast on other things. Fasting is not an end in itself. It is a means.

R.L. - Do you plow well on the fasting days?

I - On those days, the farther you are from the house and the kitchen, the better it is.

R.L. - Did the Holy Virgin talk to you about drugs?

I - Not directly, but She asks that we abandon addictions - alcohol for example. The media can also be a drug.

R.L. - How do you feel about the Serbs?

I - It is hard to say in the actual situation. But we all try to follow the Gospel, not to fixate on the people who are making the war, because it is a war between good and evil. It is not a war between men, but between God and the Devil.

R.L. - But will the Holy Virgin win?

I - Yes, without doubt. But we must be the Holy Virgin's tools if we want Her plan to work.

R.L. - The Holy Virgin told Vicka that we must love the Serbs. Is that possible for Croatians?

I - It is difficult; it is a matter of healing. We must try to heal our wounds. It is not that forgiveness is impossible, but it is difficult to gloss over certain things when the wounds are deep.

R.L. - What is the dominant impression of your trip to Australia and New-Zealand in January-February?

I - I found great spiritual changes in the people who came. They were very open to prayer and the messages: laymen, priests, bishops and even a cardinal.

R.L. - You are now 27. What will you do with your life? Jakov is getting married. What about you?

I - I still live with my family, and I am very busy with praying for the youth. I take care of a prayer group that is close to my heart. I try to spread Mary's messages as much as possible, here and across the world. For now, I consider it to be my mission.

7. MLADEN BULIC'S TESTIMONY

How I met Father Jozo Zovko after the torture

Father Zorza told us about a meeting between Mladen Bulic, of Medjugorje, and Father Jozo Zovko at the beginning of Zovko's incarceration which began on August 15, 1981.

In the middle of August 1981, I had been hospitalized for throat problems for 5 days. On August 25, I was at my bedroom window. I saw a militia car. Two policemen came out, holding my parish priest, Father Jozo, dressed in civil cloths. I hurried down the stairs to greet him because a week before he had been incarcerated. On the stairs I met Father Jozo with the two policemen. I moved towards him to shake his hand, but the two policemen pushed me away nervously. I noticed that the small group had stopped in the hallway, while waiting for a patient to leave the doctor's office. Father Jozo's ears were bleeding. Seeing how he was walking, I thought he would stay in a wheelchair for the rest of his life. I got closer and asked him, "How are you doing?"

He turned towards me with a smile and said, "You see."

Looking at his smile, I saw that teeth were missing. The right cheek was swollen. They had beaten him savagely.

One of the policeman came to me and said, "If you keep on talking, we will beat you too."

I did not let them intimidate me. I answered, "You cannot do anything. I am a patient, and I have the right to be here!"

Father Jozo went into the doctor's office with the policemen. When he came out, he asked me, "How are things going in Medjugorje?"

I answered, "All is well. Do not worry."

A policeman said, "There is nothing to worry about because tonight we'll cut his head off."

I answered, "You cannot do anything to him; you were able to beat him up; you cannot kill him."

At that point, Father Jozo turned his head and told me to be silent because it was dangerous to talk. Afterwards I learned that ten days later, the policeman who had beaten him died of a heart attack. The main policeman was telling Father Jozo that he was an enemy of the State and the government, and that he would be worn thin, and that they would get him a little bit at a time. That policeman had chained him and had put weights on his arms and legs to hurt him. But when, in the morning, they came back to take Father Jozo, they found him freed of his chains; and his cell, which did not have a lamp, was illuminated.

Now, when Father Jozo comes to Medjugorje, he stops at my home and jokes, "You see they have not killed me yet; I still have my head on my shoulders."

8. INTERVIEW WITH FATHER PETAR LJUBICIC,

FRANCISCAN: May 9, 1992
Extracts of the interview published by Stella Maris,
February 1993, no. 279

Father Petar (or Pero) Ljubicic was chosen by Mirjana for the revelation of the secrets on the day that the Gospa authorizes it. Here are some of the most significant extracts of the interview on May 9, 1992:

Question - How is the situation in Medjugorje?
P - Right now, it is calm. The war rages all around - Mostar, Capljina and Siroki Brijeg - but not in Medjugorje. Mostar, Capljina and Siroki Brijeg are targets; already 30,000 bombs have fallen. Many houses have been destroyed. The people are not afraid here. They are prepared for this situation; they are very calm because of prayer and the apparitions [...].
Q - How does the parish live in the state of war?
P - The priests are not numerous. Three fathers have gone with those who took refuge on the coast, in Mararska, and in Split, and are at the disposition of those who had to run away. Almost all the inhabitants of Mostar have left. It is the same for the villages around Medjugorje. In Medjugorje, only a few women and children have left the village. As for us, three priests remained in Medjugorje. One takes care of the young soldiers who defend the territorial limits of Medjugorje, as well as the villages which have not yet been attacked. We celebrate mass in the presbyter basement. 150 to 200 people come, sometimes even 300. On Sunday, we celebrate 3 to 4 masses. People are starting to seriously think about the invitation extended by the Gospa for the last 11 years. Now, many realize that If we had better welcomed and lived the message of conversion, prayer, fasting, penance and love, like at the beginning, we would still be in peace and joy. [...]

Q - Have the secrets of Medjugorje already happened?

P - I talked with each of the visionaries. They do not link what is happening now and the secrets. These are just the first signs, maybe the last call of Heaven to all men so that they convert. They consider this distress and suffering a moral purification, so that in the end, we believe in a God who acts. We cannot impose on Him which way to act. God offers us numerous signs so that we will believe and start a new life. Here is how I see the situation. The secrets will happen at the predicted time, the visionaries affirm. But nothing in the present events is part of the secrets. That is all we can say.

Q - You have been chosen to reveal the secrets when the time comes. How did you welcome that mission? [...]

P - I accepted it. If that is the way it must be, then it must be. I feel no weight so far, probably because many pray for this, or because God blesses me with a special grace. In any case, if I can serve as a tool in God's hand, I will not run away from this responsibility. I regret that we do not better use these signs God has given us up until now, that we do not use them better for our formation and personal growth in faith and prayer.

Q - What would you say to those who seriously welcome the Gospa's messages in Medjugorje?

P - Any man who is receptive must be grateful to God for the gift he has received. God is pure love and never really abandons us. I see the difficult situation we live now as a grace from God. The Very High is so close to us that we can feel and experience His proximity. We bear Him in our heart. That is why I want to tell all that there is no room for fear and even less for deception. We must trust God. He takes us on the reliable way to Redemption. These days are our Holy Friday. For the adversaries, this day was His failure; but in truth, it was His great and powerful victory that was starting. Our day of victory will come too. [...] surely in the near future. Mary's Immaculate Heart must triumph. Our Lady announced it. She has so many souls which searched for God's glory and gave themselves to Him through

Her. [...] Their number grows day by day. The Queen of Peace will accomplish what She came for in Medjugorje and many other places. That is why we must be happy as of now, because one day we will have a part in the joy and happiness that awaits us. For this it is worth it to abandon everything and to convert. (Stella Maris, Hauteville, Switzerland, February 1993).

9. VICKA'S INTERVIEW

BY LISE BARIL LECLERC, June 1992
Extracts

Lise Baril Leclerc, author of a book on Medjugorje, found Vicka at work at a neighbor's, with a group talking about the problems of the war. She listens, she encourages and she communicates her joy. Vicka's answers are particularly significant about her mission.

Lise Baril Leclerc - How do you manage to encourage your people in these difficult times?

Vicka - Everybody has pretty limited needs. But our presence among them makes a lot of sense to them. So it is very important that I live here in the midst of my people. Because they say, "Since Vicka has remained in Medjugorje, it is certain that nothing terrible will happen." They know very well that planes could drop bombs and fire at everything, but because some of us [visionaries] stay here, they have a certain sense of security. It does not have to be me. It could be another one, and it would be the same. However, by our presence, the people from here feel a particular security [...]

L - What must be the essential of our prayer?

V - To ask for peace, joy and love for the heart of man. Because the greatest war is in the heart of man. [...] When the heart is overcome by hate and sin, if we remove this sin and hate from our heart, then the war on the outside will stop. [...]

131

L - It is hard to practice it towards the Serbs who attack you.

V - *Bah! Yes, we are under attack. But we must love each man in spite of it because Our Lady says She is the Mother of ALL people and She loves ALL of them equally. People, my people, who understand what Our Lady means, must not give the example of sin by judging our aggressors or condemning them in any way. Only God can judge.*

L - You can do this for your people?

V - *You know, I worry a lot about my people. I wonder how I can help my people to become an example for others. We are at a point where we do not know how to live as neighbors with other ethnic groups. The result is that we are subjected to air raids. The Church is being bombed. Innocent people are dying.*

Thus, I ask my people to be patient, to truly be a model for those who attack.

10. MIRJANA FOR PEACE

On March 25, A. Bonifacio asked Mirjana what to do for peace. Her answer is surprising, especially when she talks about the Moslems' attacks and the international press attributing these attacks to the Croatians. But in Mostar and surrounding areas, it really is the Moslems who are on the offensive, even after a time of fraternization with the Croatians who had helped them.

Bonifacio - What can we do for peace?

Mirjana - *Pray to God so that He gives us the strength to spread peace to all. Pray more for our enemies so that God will help them to understand what is right and what is not. Do not judge or hate. Pray. We must look at them like lost brothers.*

B - How do you live the actual tragedy of the fights between Croatians and Moslems in Konjic?

M - *As a Croatian I have suffered before under the hand of*

Communism. It taught me that the one who bears the cross on earth will go to Paradise, and that without a cross you cannot go to Paradise. That is why I think that we Croatians are God's chosen people to bear the cross to help Him, before with the Serbs, now with the Moslems to whom the Croatians have given food and water, everything, and who are now killing us. We pray for them to give love. We do not want to hear, "The poor Croatians..." We feel loved by God. I pray so that there will be no hate, but it is easy to talk when you have not lost someone. It is difficult for the one who has lost his family, house, country, all...! We must especially pray for the children, they have committed no crime. And then, look at the pregnant women who were raped - it is terrible...!

B - Why don't you give us these children?

M - *Nobody wants the children to leave their home; and now in Medjugorje, Father Slavko and we have a project planned for a house for them. From hate love must be born, as the Pope said.*

B - That means people must take care of them.

M - *Sister Elvira says that her boys are capable because they have already taken care of old people. I will help too, and then people can be found! More than anything else, love is the most important.*

11. MARIJA ON MARRIAGE

INTERVIEW BY ALBERTO BONIFACIO
May 30, 1993

The interview given by Marija to the Italian television has caused strong emotions among Medjugorje's devotees. Some have written the visionary to dissuade her, thinking it was not her vocation or that her husband would take her away from Medjugorje and so on. Marija, who had thought about it for a long time before making her decision, justified it in the following interview:

Alberto Bonifacio - You had planned to enter the convent, and now you decide to marry. Why?

Marija - Each year, during the holidays, I would visit the convents; the monasteries especially attracted me. I spoke with Sisters and Mother Superiors. They told me, "When Medjugorje will be recognized, if you are in a convent, the Superior or the Bishop will tell you that you cannot receive pilgrims anymore. You will not be able to see them." Then I lived for 6 months in Parma with Tomislav in 1988. After that, I could not see my vocation clearly any more. I asked the Gospa, and She told me I was free to choose. It certainly was not a sin.

B - In Catechism you are taught "God has a design for you, and you must find your vocation." It is nice to think that the Lord has the best vocation for you in mind. We must try to understand in prayer that which is best for you.

M - Just a while ago, I did not know that marriage was a sacrament. In today's world we are ignorant in religious matters. Learning this, I thought, "Even if I do not become a nun, I will receive a sacrament everyday."

B - In Italy, on a television show, you said that the Gospa wants you to take your vows and enter the convent. Why do you decide otherwise now?

M - Today, thanks to God, there are many communities that accept families.

B - Each one of us, like yourself, is praying to understand what is the better way of life.

M - Certainly! Everyday of my life I decide what my heart feels. Certainly, to enter the convent is a greater sacrifice. I do not say I will not go; I am still open. If tomorrow I understand that my life is the convent... I spoke clearly of all of this to my friend, and we are searching for God's will with openness and prayer. Many tell me, "Marija, you must not marry", and they started praying. But I answer, "You pray. Do not stop praying. If you pray and I do not marry, that will be good because it is the Lord who judges and knows the best for me. Thus keep on pray-

ing since so often we only choose our small personal interests."

Now, I think my vocation will be the one of Marija the visionary. Even when there will be no more apparitions, my testimony will still be wanted. This testimony will not always be only for you, but for God. When I go to Heaven, I will not introduce myself as a visionary, but I will present my life with all the good and the evil, all that I have lived. (Eco. No. 104)

B. The people who asked to receive the video of the April 27-29 shows on the Italian television TG4 did not find Marija's word on her marriage. This part was eliminated. We do not know why since it is such a popular show.

WAR: LOVE YOUR ENEMIES

12

CHRONOLOGY

1992

April 9	6 bombs fall on Medjugorje.
May 4	Shelling of and fire within the Archbishop's Palace in Mostar.
May 11	Anniversary of Fatima. Apparition for Ivan. The holy Virgin asks him to have the Consecration to the Hearts of Jesus and Mary on Saturday, May 16. The message was questioned, but Ivan confirmed it. He did not confirm *the date*.
May 19	Death of Dr. Korljan, president of *the Scientific Episcopal Commission on Medjugorje*, whose conclusions were a 100% positive.
May 9-22	Vicka in Italy with Father Orec.
June 1	Marija, who was in Italy, comes to Medjugorje for 24 hours with a convoy from *Caritas*.
June 17, 11:30	Jozo Zovko meets John Paul II, who tells him, *"Protect Medjugorje, I am with you. I bless you. Have courage. [...] I know of your suffering in this war."* (E 112)

June 24	2,000 pilgrim peace march, guided by the visionaries. Monsignor Franic celebrates mass in Medjugorje.
June 25	Celebration of the eleventh anniversary. 7th annual apparition of the Gospa to Ivanka. 7:00 p.m. - the anniversary mass presided by Father Ivan Sevo, guardian of a neighbor convent, whose church was completely destroyed.
June 29	Ivan invites the pilgrims to the apparition of Monday June 29 on the hill of Podbrodo, where the following dialogue occurs:

The Gospa - *Dear children, abandon yourself to me completely. Give me all your problems, difficulties and start living my messages. Pray, because right now I need your prayer.*

Ivan - *We give you all our suffering and pain. You will take better care of them than we will! And on our side, we will take care of your intentions and plans. May it result in victory for You and us.*

July 27	Centennial of the parish of Medjugorje.
July 5-14	Sister Emmanuel in France.
July 31-Aug. 6	4th annual meeting of the Youth in Medjugorje.

August 5	*France - three* television shows on Medjugorje; the camps in Doboy, from where a young girl successfully escaped.
August 12	Vicka leaves for Switzerland for a medical check-up. (E 125)
August 19	Ivanka and her family leave for the USA for a month.
August 27	Ivan leaves for England with Father Slavko for reunions, testimonies and prayer. (E 129)
August 30	Medjugorje's men, who are mobilized permanently, are called for a defensive operation on the front line. (E 134)
September 13	Sunday, Celebration of the Cross. The Holy Virgin tells Ivan that this year, like the previous ones, she will stop her apparitions on the two hills (Monday and Friday) for 3 weeks.
September 14	Monsignor Ratko Peric, adjutant to Monsignor Zanic, is ordained bishop in Neum. (E 135) Soon after, interview of the new bishop by the journal *Dalmacia Slobodna*.
September 23	Ivanka comes back from Italy with her husband and daughter Mirjana, after more than one year's absence. All the visionaries are in Medjugorje, except Jakov, who remained in Italy .(E 140)

October 2	Ivan leaves for the USA.
October 8	Beginning of Ivan's visit to Canada. (E 138)
October 12	Father Slavko and Marija leave for Spain. (E 151)
October 15	Marija goes back to Medjugorje. (E 145a)
Oct. 22-25	T. Vlasic organizes a retreat for 200 "Souls offered" in sacrifice, in Montesilvano (Pescara, Italy, Eco 98).
November 4	200 Spanish Blue Helmets move into the Medjugorje bungalows for 6 months.
November 12	Marija and Father Slavko leave for Spain and Portugal through Italy.
End of November	Vicka is in Lourdes, where she receives her apparition discreetly; Marija is in Fatima.
December 8	Alberto Bonifacio and his collaborators arrive in Medjugorje under a terrible rain with 38 trucks which have been driven for 28 hours (one of Bonifacio's numerous trips, being dedicated full time to Medjugorje). Many French, English, German and American pilgrims. All the visionaries are here, except Ivan. Many soldiers attend mass.

Mid-December | Ivan comes back from America.

December 25 | 1,000 children take refuge in Medjugorje and the neighboring villages. 1,200 Christmas gifts are distributed; 1,500 pilgrims are welcomed; the Church is packed for the Midnight Mass.

December 31 | An article in Paris-Match, very favorable towards Medjugorje: a swallow that will soon bring the Spring to *La Croix* and *Le Monde* who are not predisposed to end their plot of silence.

1993

January 17 | Father Slavko and Ivan leave with Milona of Hapsburg for a conference and prayer tour of Australia, New Zealand and the Philippines.

January 20 | 4:40 p.m. arrival in Melbourne (then Sydney on the 27 and other towns; New Zealand February 5; again Melbourne, February 8; Sidney and return through Singapore, Frankfort and Vienna on February 23. More than 100,000 people attended these numerous conferences. Cardinal Glancy presided at the Sydney reunion.

January 25 | One of Alberto Bonifacio's convoys, which left from Salanges on January 18 for Sibenik through active war zones, arrives without trouble. Sibenik is only

	six kilometers away from the front line and has been subjected to widespread destruction.
February 2	Marija, instead of Vicka, leaves for Brazil with Father Leonardo Orec; warm welcome from Cardinal Sales in Cathedral in Rio de Janeiro.
February 4	First meeting between Monsignor Peric, new Bishop in Mostar, and Father Ivan Landeka, parish priest of Medjugorje. -What do you expect from me? The Bishop asked. -To be yourself, Father Ivan answered.
February 24	Father Slavko and Ivan return to Medjugorje. Marija returns for the next day's message.
March 12-15	My 28th pilgrimage to Medjugorje with Master Fricoteaux (through Venice, 16 hours by bus to reach Medjugorje, then by boat where the road cuts off; return route the same; trip detailed in *Chretiens Magazine* No. 60.)
March 18	Annual apparition to Mirjana on her birthday.
March 19	The Italian Alberto Bonifacio's pilgrimage wishes Father Jozo Slavko a happy birthday and meets high level political figures of Bosnia-Hercegovina in Mostar.

They return through Kojic, another town destroyed by shelling. The pilgrimage stops for two days on their return from Pag Island.

April 7   Spontaneously positive article from *La Croix*. It was preceded by an article in *La France Catholique*... which had previously refused to publish my articles on Medjugorje under the pretext of grave and confidential objections!

April 8   Maundy Thursday - Marija returns from Italy.

April 9   Good Friday - Large crowd on the hill for Ivan's apparition which invites us to decide for God. He leaves the next day.

April 15-18   T. Vlasic preaches to annual meeting of prayer leaders (1,200 people) 30 kilometers away from Pescara.

April 26   Marija leaves again "for a program in Italy".

April 28   Positive article in *Le Monde*: Medjugorje, "protected zone" by the Holy Virgin.

April 27-29   Marija is interviewed on Italian TV every afternoon. She announces her marriage to Paolo Lunetti.

May 2   In the "damaged" Cathedral of Mostar, Monsignor Peric and the Franciscan Provincial celebrate a mass of reconciliation and cooperation, founded on the Franciscan's unconditional obedience.

May 14 Ivanka and Mirjana leave for America to participate in the May 28-30 conference.

May 15 Monsignor Peric comes to Medjugorje to celebrate mass for Arturo Munoz, a Blue Helmet hurt in Mostar and deceased in Spain as a result of his wounds.

May 18 Meeting between Croatian President Tudman and Moslem leader Alija Izetbegovic to seek an agreement on the Vance Owen plan; no success.

May 28-30 *Fourth International Medjugorje Conference at Notre Dame University* (Indiana, USA) Monsignor Hnilica presiding, with Father Petar, Ivan, Ivanka and Mirjana.

May 29-30 Cardinal Etchegaray visits Monsignor F. Komarica, Bishop of Banja Luka, in an "ethnic cleansing" zone, where his people consisting of 92,500 Catholics are already considerably reduced. Monsignor Komarica is the President of the investigation commission on Medjugorje, which officially recognized the cult and pilgrimage on October 21, 1990. (LN 10)

June 6 Monsignor Peric comes to celebrate the Confirmation in Medjugorje.

June 24	New peace march from Humac (Franciscan convent) to Medjugorje (15 km). Starts at 11:00 a.m. with Monsignor Franic who celebrates the evening mass. Each national group is asked to bring their country's banner to honor the Gospa. The initiative comes from Germany, like in 1992.
June 25	12th anniversary of the first apparition on the hill; 8th annual apparition for Ivanka.
August 1-5	Youth festival in Medjugorje.